SOMERSET'S
BUSES

SOMERSET'S BUSES

THE STORY OF
HUTCHINGS & CORNELIUS
AND SAFEWAY SERVICES

LAURIE JAMES

TEMPUS

Published to coincide with the passing of twenty-five years since Hutchings & Cornelius Services ceased operations, and to celebrate over seventy-five years of service to the people of south Somerset by Safeway

Frontispiece: Safeway's 1949 Dennis Lancet ETP 184 was laid off in 1969 but was restored and overhauled in order to attend bus rallies. As the original registration had lapsed, it was re-registered ASV 900. Fleet engineer Joe Frost, driver Alf White and Dennis Winter proudly show off their handiwork. (Malcolm Morgan)

First published 2004

Tempus Publishing Limited
The Mill, Brimscombe Port,
Stroud, Gloucestershire, GL5 2QG
www.tempus-publishing.com

British Library Cataloguing in Publication Data.
A catalogue record for this book is available from the British Library.

ISBN 0 7524 3171 4

Typesetting and origination by Tempus Publishing Limited.
Printed in Great Britain by Midway Colour Print, Wiltshire.

Contents

Acknowledgements

A book of this type could not be written without the help and enthusiasm of many people, and I am extremely grateful to them all.

Firstly, I have drawn heavily on the material in the collection of Roger Grimley, together with his photographic archive of Hutchings & Cornelius (H&C) and Safeway. As well as being the custodian of the late Roy Lee's papers, he is an acknowledged expert on West Country independent bus operators and read the draft manuscript, making many useful suggestions and comments. Without Roger's co-operation, this project would not have been started. Photographs credited to R. Lee are reproduced by courtesy of the Roger Grimley Collection.

Records of vehicles were provided by Geoff Bruce, while Derek Persson assisted with route details and old timetables. Information, memories or photographs relating to H&C came from Gladys Alford, Dennis Single, Mrs M. Baker, Edna Dinham, Christine Hodgkinson, Bernard Welch, Charlie Dare, Cyril Thorne, John Cornelius and David Grimmett. John Hunt of Vincents allowed access to the surviving records of H&C directors' meetings. In respect of Safeway, Joe Frost recalled his lengthy time there as fleet engineer and driver, while Vernon Gunn and Jeff Rogers took time out from their busy workload to answer my questions. Jessie Osborne (Herbert Gunn's daughter) clarified certain family matters.

I must acknowledge the publications which have been consulted. Foremost among these is South Petherton Local History Group's excellent book *South Petherton in the Twentieth Century: A Village Album*, especially the sections on public transport compiled by Jo Goldie and local businesses by Pat James. Also useful were various publications and the news sheet of the PSV Circle, the South Wales and West Branch Bulletin of the Omnibus Society and various issues of *Buses* and *Buses Extra* magazines, published by Ian Allan Ltd Peter Waller of Ian Allan allowed access to their library. Also consulted was the chapter on South Petherton in the *Victoria History of the County of Somerset* by R.W. Dunning, and *The Years Between* (Volume 1) by R.J. Crawley, F.D. Simpson, and D.R. MacGregor, which tells the story of National Omnibus & Transport prior to 1930. I am very grateful to everybody at Tempus Publishing for bringing this book to fruition and finally, thanks to my wife and family who have put up with my box of 'Somerset bus junk' for so long and for suffering my occasional disappearances to South Petherton and district. To all these, and to others who have assisted in some way, I am indebted.

Producing an accurate account of a bus company's history going back to the 1920s and 1930s does have difficulties. Formal records are incomplete or lacking entirely, or memories may fade. There seem to be no details surviving of local bus service licensing matters in Yeovil or Taunton before the 1930 Road Traffic Act. Information was extracted from the material that was located, supplemented by accounts given by people who were interviewed or previously contributed to other published sources. Evidence or witness has been found in some cases to be contradictory and the reasons behind some events are probably lost as those involved are no longer with us. Naturally, any error of interpretation or omission is mine and I apologise in advance if I have inadvertently conveyed an inaccuracy.

If anyone can add to or correct anything in the book, I would be delighted if they came forward via the Publisher. Efforts have been made to give correct credit for the photographs, and to seek permission for those which have been used, but some were not labelled on the reverse, and have been attributed to 'Author's Collection'.

Laurie James
Walton-on-Thames
September 2003

This 1930s family snapshot shows Hutchings & Cornelius' Dennis Arrow Minor CYC 422 parked outside the Royal Oak at Barrington, home of the Cornelius family. In front of the coach are (left to right): Fred Bridge, Alf Cornelius, son Charlie and Mrs Cornelius. Behind it is the bus garage, which closed in 1970 when all vehicles were concentrated at South Petherton. (R. Grimley collection)

This is an official Hutchings & Cornelius publicity photograph, depicting Austin CXD (RYD 143) and underfloor-engined Dennis Lancets (TYC 319/20). (Mrs M. Baker collection)

Preface

The West Country has for long been a bastion of independent bus operation, but even more so since the 'deregulation' of the industry in 1986, although it could be argued that after the privatisation of the National Bus Co. in the middle part of the 1980s, nearly all bus companies have been 'independent'. Many small operators in the West were based in villages and ran infrequent market day services once or twice a week to the nearest important towns, often of a quite lengthy nature. The buses with which this book is concerned were provided by two companies who operated their main services six or seven days a week with some running alongside routes of the ubiquitous state-owned 'National' undertaking for considerable distances, on equal terms. More remarkable is the fact they were based in the same village in Somerset – South Petherton – and managed to co-exist harmoniously alongside each other.

Mention the words 'buses' and 'South Petherton' to many people in south Somerset and they will quickly reply 'Miss Gunn and Safeway', while those of a certain age might also say 'Hutchings & Cornelius'. The local reputation of these firms was legendary, and in the case of Safeway still is, as happily they are still with us. In the early years the need to compete effectively with National was essential for survival as many small companies simply caved in under pressure, or sold out at a relatively low price. Messrs Hutchings, Cornelius and Gunn achieved almost hero status as they managed to provide the villages with a cheaper, friendlier and more reliable bus service than that offered by National. The fact that they were local counted a lot in terms of customer loyalty and it says much that people would deliberately let the National bus go by, so they could travel with H&C or Safeway. If the driver or conductor was not actually related to you, they were probably a friend or acquaintance. People would be picked up outside their door, with the bus waiting if they were not quite ready. On the return from town, the bus could not leave until any latecomers had got back with their shopping. Yet this familiarity did not mean inefficiency. The companies provided the only means of transport for many of the inhabitants of sleepy villages scattered over the pleasant landscape along the rivers Isle and Parrett.

In terms of geographical features, the operating area of H&C and Safeway falls into two contrasting categories. From a line through Barrington, the Lambrooks and Martock, southwards to South Petherton and on towards Crewkerne and Yeovil, there is undulating farmland and many villages with buildings made from hamstone, a scene typical in many ways of classic pastoral England. Yet to the north is a large area of flatter, low-lying, wetland and pasture, punctuated by a network of drainage channels and roads on raised causeways, to which cling scattered villages and hamlets. Osier Beds were a feature, and in the old days the frequent flooding of the Levels added to the rural isolation and made for a difficult operating territory for bus services.

Yet H&C and Safeway Services are known well beyond the boundaries of Somerset. Their inclination for unusual vehicle purchase policies, at least for a small rural independent operator, coupled with the forthright views of their proprietors on the right way of running a successful local public bus service, ensured that they were well-regarded within the transport industry and also recognised by people generally interested in buses, especially those having a connoisseur's penchant for rural independents. Their reputation is a result of the great efforts of the proprietors and their loyal staff, including through difficult times.

For the historian, there are plenty of dates and facts within these pages, but buses are about people too, as people made H&C what they were and Safeway what they are, so a sprinkling of anecdotes and reminiscences is included. The material in this book includes some local research and personal observation carried out by the late Roy Lee in the 1950s and 1960s. As well as digging into the past, he made extensive notes of routes taken, vehicles operated and working practices. The material in his carefully home-produced but unpublished volumes has proved most useful. Much additional research and interviews have been undertaken to make this record more complete and it is hoped that this book will serve as tribute to those associated with the two companies, that it will appeal to various categories of reader and will bring back memories for those who know H&C and Safeway or have used their services.

Herbert and Veronica Gunn, the joint proprietors of Safeway Services from 1938 to 1977, seen in the mid-1960s. Veronica carried on alone until her death in 1999. (Commercial Motor)

Introduction

South Petherton – the village

South Petherton is a large village about six miles to the west of the industrial and market town of Yeovil and situated between there and the county town of Taunton. It is 135 miles from London down the A303, which stretches from near Basingstoke in Hampshire to north of Honiton in Devon, having been developed as an alternative to the earlier A30 through Yeovil and Chard.

Yet as the main road runs to the south of the village, South Petherton itself retains an unhurried tranquil air and at first sight might appear very much as it did, say, fifty years ago. It is five miles from the ancient market towns of Crewkerne and Ilminster, and along with Yeovil and Taunton, these places generated various travel requirements for the inhabitants of South Petherton, as we shall see later.

The parish of South Petherton is the largest in the ancient Hundred of the same name, with 'Petherton' being derived from the nearby river Parrett, which together with the river Isle meanders timelessly. The designation 'South' was added to distinguish the village from North Petherton situated further along the Parrett near Bridgwater.

The main village lies in a hollow, the highest point of the parish being only 231 feet above sea level. Much of it is on the fertile 'Yeovil Sands', but there is also a limestone ridge. This was quarried at Pitway in the nineteenth century to produce Petherton Stone. Attractive honeyed-stone buildings are a feature of the village and others in the area. There are villages around which have, to the outsider, enchanting names such as Montacute, Stoke Sub Hamdon, Haselbury Plucknett, Curry Rivel and Isle Abbotts, and more intriguing still, Kingsbury Episcopi.

The present settlement of South Petherton is probably of Saxon origin, and rising above the village is the fine octagonal tower of St Peter and St Paul's parish church. Nearby runs the main St James Street, lined with shops and houses and joined by a network of small sidestreets. Although the core of the village has altered little, there has been some housing development nearby, especially in the last fifty years. In 1991 the population was recorded as 3,100 (30 per cent more than in 1891) and no doubt this will rise when the results of the 2001 census are released.

It is recorded that in 1950 South Petherton was 'a community of typical West Country folk, with a few London evacuees who decided to stay after the war. Nearly everyone was related to someone or other and most people were engaged in agriculture or glove-making'. Since then, as in many places, the importance of agriculture has declined and is far less labour-intensive. Some people have moved away but others have arrived, being engaged in a variety of occupations, including light industry or commerce in the

The centre of H&C administration for about fifty years was Cornhill House in The Square, South Petherton, as well as being home to members of the Hutchings, Cornelius and Alford families. It is now purely a private residence. (J. Cornelius)

surrounding area. For a long time, the Westlands Aircraft Factory at Yeovil was a significant local employer and some worked at the Isolation Hospital opened in 1938, which is now used for more general medical and care purposes.

In the beginning

In passenger transport terms, the twentieth century caught up with South Petherton in 1919 when Bill Gayleard bought a solid-tyred open charabanc. Bill was part of a well known local family and was a saddler, bill poster and Town Crier. His father had been in charge of the horse-drawn fire engine kept at the Blake Memorial Hall in The Square, a building erected in 1911 on the corner of St James Street to replace the previous Market Hall. This charabanc which was used for local outings to the seaside must have been a feat of endurance with a bumpy ride on metalled but un-tarmacked roads, but horizons were broadened and people's outlook on life began to be changed. Before then, only short trips could be made in horse-drawn wagonettes or farm carts, and the nearest station was at Martock on the line from Taunton and Langport to Yeovil. The Carrier's Cart was a vital mode of transport for getting goods to and from the surrounding towns.

It seems that the first bus service for South Petherton started in 1920, when Mr Bates, trading as White Bros and Bates, put a green fourteen-seater onto a route from the village to Yeovil via Montacute. It is remembered that a Mr Barnes was the driver and Mr Bates the conductor, with the bus being kept in the yard of the Crown Hotel, off The Square, where Mr Rathers, the proprietor, had previously hired out horses, carriages and wagonettes, as well as keeping racehorses. Previous to activities in Somerset, White Bros and Bates were based at Sherborne St John in Hampshire, where they ran a service from Basingstoke to Newbury for at least three months from November 1919. Bates sold out to National on 5 July 1920, thus giving that rapidly growing concern a toehold in the Yeovil area. The bus was fairly new, being a chain-driven vehicle of Commer manufacture, but as it was somewhat noisy was soon replaced by National with a AEC YC type twenty-four-seater, which had started life as an open-top double-decker at their Shepherd's Bush garage. Drivers Papworth, Brown and Crittle came down from London with it, to establish a small operation, which was how National worked its away across the West Country.

'National' was the National Omnibus and Transport Co. Ltd, which originated in London in 1909 as the National Steam Car Co. before expanding into the northern London suburbs, Hertfordshire, Bedfordshire and East Anglia and then on to the West Country. They soon extended the South Petherton route to Ilminster and moved the bus to a covered garage in Butt Lane which was rented from Mr Walter of 'Roundwell'. The Ilminster service was numbered 1 (later renumbered 21 and then Southern National service 6) while new routes were opened from Yeovil to Ash, Martock and Bower Hinton, numbered 4 (later renumbered 25 and then Southern National service 14), and from Yeovil to Crewkerne via West Coker, numbered 3, later 22 and Southern National 7.

Until the late 1960s, this device was the logo of Hutchings & Cornelius, appearing on the sides of the vehicles. (Author's collection)

It is 1947 and glum faces all round as striking H&C staff are addressed by a union representative, who is standing on the barrel in the yard of the Wyndham Arms at Kingsbury Episcopi. Among the strikers are: Charlie Brown, Fred Bridge, Cyril Welch, Reg Beale, Fred Welch, Edna Dinham, Jack Bindon, Harry Quantock, Howard Drayton, Fred Virgin, Len Hooper, Dick Ryder, Bert Gass and Bill Harwood. (Mrs M. Baker collection)

During 1929, National's West Country operations were divided between the Western National Omnibus Co. Ltd (in the area covered predominantly by the Great Western Railway) and the Southern National Omnibus Co. Ltd (in the mainly Southern Railway territory). This followed a substantial investment by these railway companies in National Omnibus & Transport. The Southern National entity disappeared in January 1971 when it was part of the state-owned National Bus Co., being merged into Western National, but became separate again in 1983 as a prelude to the privatisation of National Bus Co. subsidiaries.

National moved their South Petherton-based buses in 1938 to 'the Institute', also known as 'the Drill Hall' in Crown Lane, a large wooden building which they bought from the church authorities. When it stopped being used operationally, it became a store for withdrawn vehicles and was demolished in 1999 in favour of two houses. The various National companies and their direct successor have operated through South Petherton and district until the present day, but that, as they say, is another story.

Hutchings & Cornelius
Services Ltd

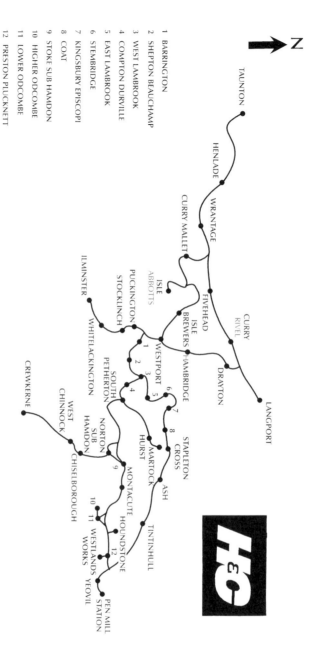

N

HUTCHINGS & CORNELIUS BUS SERVICES

H3C

TAUNTON
HENLADE
WRANTAGE
CURRY MALLET
FIVEHEAD
CURRY RIVEL
DRAYTON
LANGPORT
ISLE ABBOTTS
ISLE BREWERS
ILMINSTER
PUCKINGTON
STOCKLINCH
WHITELACKINGTON
WESTPORT
HAMBRIDGE
SOUTH PETHERTON
STAPLETON CROSS
NORTON SUB HAMDON
MARTOCK
ASH
CREWKERNE
WEST CHINNOCK
CHISELBOROUGH
MONTACUTE
HOUNDSTONE
TINTINHULL
WESTLANDS WORKS
YEOVIL
PEN MILL STATION

1 BARRINGTON
2 SHEPTON BEAUCHAMP
3 WEST LAMBROOK
4 COMPTON DURVILLE
5 EAST LAMBROOK
6 STEMBRIDGE
7 KINGSBURY EPISCOPI
8 COAT
9 STOKE SUB HAMDON
10 HIGHER ODCOMBE
11 LOWER ODCOMBE
12 PRESTON PLUCKNETT

one
Thomas Hutchings of South Petherton

It seems to have been in 1926 that Thomas Hutchings formalised his passenger-carrying activities while living in a house on the corner of Palmer Street and St James Street, opposite the Coke Memorial Methodist church at the end of North Street. At the side of the house was a small garage, from where it is probable that he ran a 1922 Chevrolet with around eight seats, registered YA 4505, although this may not have been formally defined as a Public Service Vehicle. This was accompanied by YB 895, a fourteen-seat Chevrolet which had been first registered in February 1925.

Hutchings started a service on Mondays to Saturdays from South Petherton to Yeovil, terminating near the Pen Mill Station of the Great Western Railway. It ran through Stoke Sub Hamdon, Montacute, Preston and Yeovil town centre with some journeys later being

Seen in recent times, this is the house on the corner of Palmer Street and St James Street in South Petherton where Tommy Hutchings lived in the 1920s when he started his passenger-carrying business. (Author)

YC 7987 was a Thornycroft BC with thirty-two-seat bodywork by Ransomes, Simms & Jefferies, new to Hutchings in December 1929. It is seen in Seaton with one of Dunns of Taunton's Leylands behind. The roof-mounted advertising board extols the virtues of West's Drapers of Yeovil, offering 'unrivalled quality'. (J. Fielder/R. Marshall collection)

diverted to serve Norton Sub Hamdon, and a Sunday afternoon service being introduced. Journeys were also diverted at the appropriate times to serve the Westlands Aircraft Factory on the outskirts of Yeovil. The level of service to and from Yeovil was increased when a second service was introduced on Mondays to Saturdays, from Chiselborough, and joining the original service at Stoke Sub Hamdon. Most journeys on this service did not run on Thursdays, early closing day in Yeovil. As an example, the return fare from South Petherton to Yeovil at this time was 1s 6d (7.5 pence in modern currency).

The advent of another bus service for South Petherton and the other villages further increased people's ability to get easily to a major town to obtain goods or attend the market, not available locally. In the days before television, a visit to the theatre or cinema became a social occasion, and evening departures from Yeovil were timed to coincide with the end of performances. The number of people travelling on Hutchings' buses often exceeded their proper capacity and it probably came as a relief when he purchased a new twenty-seat Thornycroft A2L in November 1927. The fourteen-seat Chevrolet, having been sold to Alfred Cornelius of Barrington, returned to the fleet before being replaced by a fourteen-seat Thornycroft A1 in November 1928. To cope with the expanded services, a twenty-six-seat Thornycroft A6 was purchased new in June 1929, followed five months later by a forward-control thirty-two-seat Thornycroft BC, which no doubt became the pride of the fleet.

By 1930, Hutchings had moved to Cornhill House in The Square, and was trading as Hutchings Omnibus Service, as well as running taxis for general hire. The vehicles were liveried cream with black lining, and were kept in premises at the rear of Cornhill House, in Crown Lane, almost opposite the Southern National garage.

Before the implementation of the Road Traffic Act of 1930, bus services were usually only licensed by local councils in the larger towns. Competition between operators was unregulated and was certainly fierce on the Yeovil routes, where the National company probably regarded Hutchings as an interloper. Predatory tactics usually came from the larger company and often developed into a race to get to the intending passengers first. On one occasion, the National and Hutchings buses were so busy trying to get in front of each other that some passengers were missed altogether!

The Road Traffic Act required all bus services to be licensed by a regulator, known as the Traffic Commissioner, who would decide which services should run, at what level and by whom. When competing applications were received, he could hold a hearing at a Traffic Court, where operators could be legally represented to protect their interests, and could lodge objections to the plans of others. Having been presented with all the evidence, the Commissioner would then make a ruling, and the successful applicant could then start their service. Somerset falls in the Western Traffic Area and operators began making formal application for their existing services in the spring of 1931. Most services already running were usually authorised under 'grandfather rights', including those of Hutchings. However, he had to lodge a timetable and then maintain it fully, and could not make changes to deal with new circumstances without going back to the Commissioner, or adjust the timings on a whim to get in front of the Southern National service.

Driver Fred Virgin poses alongside Thornycroft YC 7987 in 1936, after the formation of H&C. It was in the cream and black livery of the period. Note the guard rails along the underside of the body (R. Grimley collection)

Hutchings also ran day excursions from South Petherton and Stoke sub Hamdon to various seaside resorts such as Weston-super-Mare, Weymouth and Bournemouth, and these too were licensed. Private-hire operations did not require a licence.

Despite the National and Safeway services between South Petherton and Yeovil, that of Hutchings was very popular with much local loyalty. In January 1932, Hutchings was summoned to Yeovil Police Court for being caught with forty people on a bus licensed to carry thirty-two. In his defence, he said that it was morally difficult to leave people behind on such a rural service, and had already applied for additional journeys. The bench dismissed the case on payment of four shillings costs.

In May 1933, Hutchings applied to extend the Chiselborough service to the next village – West Chinnock, and this was granted, starting by September of that year. However, this permitted expansion did not alter the fact that small bus companies like Hutchings did feel vulnerable in the face of the large conglomerates such as Southern National, who had been expanding and consolidating their hold on bus services in Somerset for some years, having bought out a number of the local 'independent' operators.

Hutchings enjoyed a good relationship with Alfred Cornelius of Barrington, which is about three miles from South Petherton. Cornelius was another small bus proprietor, of which more anon, facing similar problems, and the two decided to merge so as to combine their resources in an attempt to keep Southern National at bay. At the same time, they sought additional backing from an outside source in order to strengthen their position, and the combined undertaking was registered as Hutchings and Cornelius Services Ltd on 31 May 1934.

two
Alfred Cornelius & Sons of Barrington

The landlord of the Royal Oak Inn, situated in the main street at Barrington, was Alfred Cornelius, and early in 1928 he started a bus service from Shepton Beauchamp to Taunton, via Barrington, Westport, Hambridge, Curry Rivel, Fivehead, Wrantage and Henlade. Initially, only one round trip was operated with a fourteen-seat Chevrolet which was purchased from Thomas Hutchings. It was kept in the yard behind the inn. Alfred Cornelius had three sons – Charlie and Len were involved in the bus business but Stan was a builder.

Len Cornelius drove one of the first journeys to Taunton, blissfully unaware that he should have had a licence from the local council to drive in that town. The policeman from Ilminster tipped him off, and then he duly applied and had to take a driving test, following which police Inspector Chapman passed him.

Also owned was a Ford Model T car first registered in April 1922, and used for general hire. It disgraced itself on one occasion by catching fire while taking people to the Jordan point-to-point races near Ilminster. Alfred Cornelius had a smallholding and Fred Bridge remembered driving a round trip to Taunton on occasions, and then helping out on the smallholding until it was time for the next journey. The telephone number at the Royal Oak was Ilminster 55Y4, in the quaint numbering system of the time and the Cornelius family were much involved in passing messages for the local community as it was one of the very few telephones in the Barrington area.

After about six months, the Chevrolet was sold back to Hutchings, as in May 1928, Cornelius took delivery of a new Thornycroft A2 bus with a twenty-seat Vincent body. The following year the fleet doubled with the arrival of a new fourteen-seat Chevrolet, with bodywork by Marks Bros of Wilton which featured a canvas roof. Some land adjacent to the inn was purchased and a bus garage built there, with a skittle alley at the rear. When the skittle alley was moved later to behind the inn, the space for buses was extended.

The Taunton service saw an increase in journeys and was diverted via Drayton and a double run was introduced along the A378 to serve the town of Langport. A service from Barrington to Yeovil was started, running via Shepton Beauchamp, West Lambrook, Stembridge, Kingsbury Episcopi, Coate, Stapleton Cross, Ash and Tintinhull, running each weekday except Thursday. It soon encountered competition from Sully's Yeovil service, while the Cornelius service to Taunton had to contend with National service 5 which ran from Taunton to Yeovil via Langport, Somerton and Ilchester, and was later numbered 264. One day, Len Cornelius overtook a National bus, and the next time he stopped for passengers, the National driver caught up and threatened to 'knock his door off'. Such ripostes were not uncommon, and at one time, National sent down two inspectors from their London operation to help the local staff get one better on the small

Alf Cornelius' third vehicle was this fourteen-seat Marks-bodied Chevrolet LQ, new in August 1929. Note the canvas roof which was able to be rolled back on fine days. Although still in Cornelius two-tone blue livery, it is seen here when owned by Mr Watts of Isle Brewers. The flooding was an occupational hazard in those parts in the 1930s. (R. Grimley collection)

On a private hire job or an excursion to Seaton is YD 4044, a fine Thornycroft Cygnet with Beadle body bought by Alf Cornelius in February 1932. The monogram on the rear later developed into a similar device for H&C, and note the early telephone number 'Ilminster 55Y4'. (J. Fielder)

Seen later in its life, Thornycroft Cygnet YD 9639 carries a mainly cream livery, lined black, and a different style of H&C fleet name on the side. Parked at Barrington, opposite the garage, it is attended to by a cleaning party. (R. Grimley collection)

companies. Sometimes, Sully or Cornelius buses would find themselves sandwiched between two National vehicles.

F. Sully and Sons of Horton started vigorous competition with National between Chard, Ilminster and Taunton in October 1928. The following year, they started a service from Ilminster to Yeovil via Barrington, Shepton Beauchamp, Kingsbury Episcopi, Martock, Stoke Sub Hamdon and Montacute, running on Mondays, Tuesdays, Wednesdays, Fridays and Saturdays. This competed with Cornelius but also Hutchings between Stoke and Yeovil. Sully's was quite a nuisance, and eventually sold out to Southern National in April 1936. The latter numbered the Yeovil service 91, but it did not endure.

Cornelius vehicles were painted two shades of blue. The fleet expanded with the addition of further Vincent-bodied Thornycrofts in 1930 and 1931. Vincents were a firm based in Yeovil, also being motor traders, and were to figure in larger measure later in the Hutchings & Cornelius story. In February 1932 came YD4044, a six-cylinder-engined Thornycroft Cygnet with a thirty-two-seat Beadle rear-entrance bodywork, being the first forward-control bus in stock.

There is a story told that in the early 1930s, Alf Cornelius went to the Thornycroft factory in Basingstoke to collect a new bus. By the time he had driven it back as far as Salisbury, he discovered a defect which did not please him. He therefore went into the nearest branch of his bank and stopped his payment cheque, presumably as a prelude to a dialogue with Thornycrofts about rectification!

Some time before the applications for service licences under the Road Traffic Act were made in June 1931, the Yeovil service was extended from Barrington to Puckington and Ilminster. It was subsequently diverted via Stocklinch and Whitelackington after a resident of Stocklinch asked Alf Cornelius to do so on the spur of the moment one rainy day. Both the Yeovil and Taunton services were allowed to continue. A year later, a successful application was made to run journeys back to Barrington at 11 p.m., to cater for returning cinema-goers from Taunton and Ilminster on Saturday evenings. By the start of 1933, the Taunton service had two journeys each way on Mondays to Fridays, and four inward and five outward journeys on Saturdays. Also introduced was a Saturday route variant between Barrington and Taunton, via Westport, Isle Brewers, Fivehead and Curry Mallet, then joining the main route east of Wrantage. The bus departed from Barrington at 9.45 a.m., returning from Taunton at 2 p.m.

A successful application in June 1933 saw the diversion of the Yeovil service via East Lambrook. This route then had two trips each way on Mondays, Tuesdays, Wednesdays and Fridays and four on Saturdays, as well as 'short' journeys between Barrington and Ilminster. At this time, a new thirty-two-seat Dennis Lancet coach was purchased at a cost of £1,000, the first Thornycroft being traded in against it. From 22 July 1933, the Taunton service was extended from Shepton Beauchamp through to South Petherton via West Lambrook and Compton Durville, and some extra journeys introduced between Barrington and South Petherton, which were licensed separately. The return fare from South Petherton to Taunton was 2s 6d (12.5 pence). Finally, in spring 1934 a Sunday Ilminster–Barrington–South Petherton service was authorised with five journeys each way, connecting at South Petherton with the Hutchings service to Yeovil. Following the meeting of the services of Messrs Cornelius and Hutchings, the stage was set for the full integration of the two operators.

three
Unification and consolidation

The name Vincent has already appeared as a bus bodybuilder, and was a long-established family concern. John Vincent was trading as a wheelwright by 1840, at Wayford near Crewkerne and subsequently at Clapton. By the turn of the century their coachwork activities employed about 100 people with premises in Yeovil. John Vincent's grandson James was joined in the business by the latter's son Stanley in 1909 and together they saw the transition from the horse-drawn era to the internal combustion engine.

They developed extensive car showrooms and motor repair workshops, culminating in the opening of new premises in 1930 by Sir Herbert Austin, the founder of the Austin Motor Co. In 1932 Stanley bought land to create Yeovil's first purpose-built car park and went on to build a two-storey car park for cinema patrons and those attending the market.

Thus it was that Stanley Vincent became involved with Alf Cornelius and Tom Hutchings with also a tangible interest in their new combined business. Hutchings & Cornelius Services Ltd was registered on 31 May 1934, with a capital of £1,000, with these three being the directors, and a registered office at Vincent Chambers in Yeovil.

This is an official Works Photograph of H&C Thornycroft Cygnet YD 9639. The handsome Beadle body offered superior comfort to that of vehicles of National at that time. Originally used by Thornycroft as a demonstration model, it had appeared at the Commercial Motor Show at Olympia, before joining H&C in May 1934. (R. Grimley collection)

CYC 657 was a twenty-six-seat all-Dennis Arrow Minor of 1937 which lasted in the fleet until 1953. The photograph was taken in Ilchester, away from H&C's bus-operating area. (J. Parke/Omnibus Society)

The firm's administrative headquarters were at Cornhill House in South Petherton, and both depots were retained. The one in Crown Lane in South Petherton held four or five vehicles, and more could be parked in a yard further along the same road. The Royal Oak garage at Barrington held nine vehicles, so overall there was room for fleet expansion. The bus services were operated very much as before the merger, with South Petherton depot responsible for the main routes to Yeovil from there and West Chinnock, and Barrington depot supplying the buses for the routes to Ilminster, Taunton and the 'roundabout' Yeovil service. School transport contracts continued to run to Stoke sub Hamdon, Yeovil and other places, also the advertised excursions started by Hutchings.

The initial fleet consisted of four Hutchings Thornycrofts, and three from Cornelius, as well as his Dennis Lancet. Another Beadle-bodied Thornycroft Cygnet arrived in May 1934, having previously been a demonstration vehicle which had been exhibited at the Commercial Motor Show at Olympia in London. This was followed two months later by the arrival of a new twenty-seat Dennis Ace, registered AYA 170, being the first in the fleet with a registration mark which commenced with three letters. The chosen livery for the combined operation was cream and black, probably similar to that of Hutchings.

The first bus service developments after the merger came on 1 August 1934, when timetable modifications were introduced on a number of services. These included the Taunton via Isle Brewers and Curry Mallet service which was increased to run Mondays to Saturdays. Apart from some timetable changes, the services then remained very similar until after the war. However, by the latter part of the decade, storm clouds were gathering over Europe, accompanied by various preparations and a military build-up in Britain. In 1939, Houndstone Camp was opened on the outskirts of Yeovil, near Preston and quite close to the H&C South Petherton–Yeovil service, on which some journeys were diverted to serve the camp.

Before the war, H&C acquired six more vehicles with a seating capacity of twenty to twenty-six. Bought new were a Dennis Mace, which had a centre-entrance body disliked by some conductors, two Thornycroft Daintys and two Dennis Arrow Minors. There was also a second-hand Dennis GL bought from a firm in Aylesbury, and seemingly only lasting about a year with H&C. These vehicles permitted the withdrawal of the three oldest Thornycrofts inherited from Hutchings.

In the 1930s, the daily takings were sent by H&C bus from South Petherton or Barrington to Yeovil, where staff at Vincents' office would then take them to the bank.

In June 1939, the H&C fleet stood at thirteen Dennis and Thornycroft vehicles, which had run 216,000 miles in the previous twelve-month period, with receipts of around £11,500. The management of Southern National based in Exeter investigated H&C for possible purchase, but this was not progressed as they were too busy making preparations for the forthcoming emergency situation.

Pictured during the Second World War at Taunton is AOR 147, a Wadham-bodied Thornycroft Dainty of 1935. Notable is the green/brown livery of the period and the masked headlamps which only allowed a thin slit of light during the blackout. It survived in the fleet until 1950. (J. Parke/ Omnibus Society)

The Works photograph of a Thornycroft Dainty with full-front twenty-five-seat bodywork by Grose. It is seen in July 1936 before being registered BYD 182 and sign-written for H&C. Note that the 'legal lettering' at the bottom of the side panels shows Vincent Motors, as the order was probably made under their name on behalf of H&C. (R. Grimley collection)

four
The war years

In Somerset, as elsewhere in Britain, the war was to have a profound effect on bus and coach operators, and parts of the county did suffer the consequences of aerial attack. On one occasion a H&C Bedford WTB, registered EBB 349 was temporarily marooned near Houndstone Camp, when a German aircraft dropped a bomb in front of it, and then one behind it. It could not be moved until the crater in front had been hastily infilled. Another wartime second-hand acquisition, Dennis Lancet CUP 282 was painted brown, while other vehicles running to the Westlands factory had their roofs camouflaged to make them less visible from the air.

Great emphasis was made by the authorities on making only essential trips, and thus coaching activities for leisure purposes ceased. Fuel for private motoring was rationed and some stored their cars for the duration. There was a huge demand for bus travel and frequently H&C's small vehicles were carrying many more people than they were licensed for. Regular travellers were greatly augmented by an influx of evacuees from London and other cities and many personnel from the armed forces stationed in the area. Every

CUP 282, a Duple-bodied Dennis Lancet, was a second-hand wartime acquisition which arrived in 1941, when any vehicle was hard to obtain. Seen in Yeovil in the 1950s, shortly before it was withdrawn for re-bodying. (A. Cross)

available vehicle had to be pressed into service to cope with the demand, making little time for maintenance which was hampered by the short supply of essential spare parts, therefore shortening the life-expectancy of the relatively light-weight vehicles.

There were also staffing problems as some of the drivers and conductors had to answer an invitation to join the hostilities, and for those that remained, working life was strenuous with long shifts, nights in the depots keeping the vehicles fit for service, and no interior illumination requiring conductors to use a shaded torch clipped to their jackets so they could see to handle money and issue Bell Punch tickets from the hand-held rack. Headlamps were so severely masked as to render them next to useless, therefore accidents in the blackout were not uncommon.

At one time there was apparently a rumour of an imminent German invasion. All the Barrington depot vehicles were parked in staggered formation along the main village street, to act as a blockade!

In late 1939, H&C took delivery of a new Dennis Lancet with a thirty-three-seat Duple coach body which was ordered before the war started. Driver Osborne collected it from the supplier in London and was advised by the police to stop a while as it was thought to be an easy target to spot from the air when it was on the move! In general, though, H&C had to make do the same as most small operators, and some of the older buses were replaced with second-hand Bedford and Dennis vehicles and also a Thornycroft, some of which were just as old and would not have been up to H&C standards were it not for the wartime conditions. The Thornycroft, together with another which entered service after the war was believed to have been stored in a forest for two years, prior to arriving at H&C, being previously owned by the War Department.

An interesting acquisition was a Tilling Stevens B10C2 built in 1929 with a Short Bros rear-entrance body. Originally owned by the East Kent Road Car Co. and withdrawn by

Dennis Lancet/Duple coach EYD 220 in the 1950s with other typical coaches of the period in the background. This was ordered before the war but delivered in late 1939 after its commencement. (R. Grimley collection)

Wartime pressure on the ageing H&C fleet was relieved in January 1943 when the company was permitted to augment it with two new Bedford OWBs to a strict utility specification, which originally included wooden slatted seats. FYD 138 had Mulliner bodywork and left H&C in 1955, unlike its sister FYD 137 which enjoyed longevity in rebuilt form, having its almost identical Duple body rebuilt by Vincents in the 1950s. An August 1952 photograph. (A. Cross)

Another wartime second-hand purchase was Dennis Lancet/Duple BTE 861 which unlike CUP 282 was not re-bodied, lasting until 1958 as H&C's last half-cab vehicle. It was photographed near the garage at South Petherton. When it arrived it had a petrol engine but this was replaced with a diesel unit. It was reported to be comfortable to drive. (R. Lee)

Dennis Lancet1 JJ 1836 had been in the London Transport fleet before the war, and was new to Puttergill (Golden Arrow) of London, SW9. Alongside is Thornycroft AOR 147. They are parked at the Kings Arms terminus in Taunton in the latter part of the war, equipped with headlamp masks. (J. Parke/Omnibus Society)

them in 1939, it was purchased from another well-known Somerset independent operator, Wakes of Sparkford near Wincanton, who had not operated it. It only had brakes on the rear wheels and is thought to have been converted to an ambulance while in Kent. To restore it to passenger-carrying duty, old seats from a cinema in Yeovil were fitted around the perimeter. It was based at Barrington, where a mechanic could tune its four-cylinder engine to perfection. It was difficult to drive through the narrow lanes which were so much a feature of H&C bus routes and after the war it was transferred to South Petherton and used on the workers' journeys to the Westlands factory.

The manufacture and distribution of new buses was strictly controlled by the Government. Single-deckers meant petrol-engined Bedford OWB models with basic bodywork to a utility specification, including wooden slatted seats. Operators could only obtain them if they could demonstrate a real need, such as the provision of transport essential to the war effort. In January 1943, H&C took delivery of a pair, with thirty-two-seat bodies and registered FYD 137/138. The former was re-bodied by Vincents in the 1950s and lasted until 1967.

During the war, H&C operated a contract to carry workmen engaged in building a camp at Henstridge on the Dorset border. It started in Barrington and ran via Langport and Somerton, and was a lengthy trip for the ancient Tilling-Stevens. Workmen were also transported to the Digby Estate in Sherborne, where they were building a hospital. Mrs Alford remembers having to scrub and disinfect buses on Sundays which had been used to convey workmen building airfields at Ilton and Zeals.

Thomas Hutchings sold his interest in the company, and retired to Bournemouth, his shares being bought by Alf Cornelius, who was now Managing Director, and Stanley

The desperate wartime search for usable vehicles resulted in two elderly Thornycrofts arriving as 'stop gaps'. AHU 450 was a Cygnet model of 1934, and originated with Gough's Queen of the Road Coaches of Bristol. After use by the War Department, it had allegedly been stored in a forest prior to arriving at South Petherton. (J. Parke/Omnibus Society)

Vincent. Subsequently, Ernie Cartwright, son-in-law of Alf Cornelius became a director, while Alf's daughter Gladys and other son-in-law Fred Alford then moved into Cornhill House in South Petherton and the latter became Company Secretary. The large front room there had been converted into a booking, enquiry and administration office, as well as acting as a point for the despatch and collection of parcels conveyed by bus, which in those days was a much-used way of receiving goods from suppliers in the towns. Len Cornelius was made Foreman in charge at Barrington depot.

five
Signs of change

The period between the end of the war and the late 1950s saw continued good use made of bus services, as well as advertised day excursions and private hire which were resumed. People were keen to travel after years of keeping journeys to a minimum, and the slow availability of more goods in the shops created demand for shopping trips to large towns like Yeovil and Taunton, which meant going by bus for most.

On Saturday afternoons when the Taunton service was very popular, Barrington people would board the bus on its way out from Taunton and pay 1d to Shepton Beauchamp so as to be sure of a seat on the return journey to town. If the bus arrived at Barrington full, the driver would alert Len Cornelius who would bring out a 'relief' bus to which the conductor would transfer, and then the service bus would go non-stop via Ashill to Taunton. Buses would also wait near Hambridge, and if one was full it would cut across behind Curry Rivel and head straight for Taunton.

In 1947 some firms were once again receiving new vehicles and thus JPK 803, a Bedford/Mulliner utility bus was purchased from Sidney Hayter's Yellow Bus Service of Guildford. It stayed ten years in Somerset and was photographed in August 1952. (A. Cross)

The late-afternoon buses from Taunton were extremely popular, and several 'reliefs' were often needed. On the 4 p.m. departure, any such extras would have to wait at the Curry Mallet turn near Wrantage for the main bus serving Curry Mallet, so that those going there could transfer. If the Curry Mallet bus got there first, it would have to wait for all the 'reliefs' to arrive for this to occur. Similarly, the 6 p.m. departure to South Petherton would require up to five 'reliefs' and sometimes the police would stop them on the outskirts of Taunton to check for overloading, which was often the case. At Curry Rivel, there would be a grand sort-out of passengers, allowing some of the reliefs to run direct to Hambridge, Westport and Barrington. The 'service' bus would also cover Langport and Drayton, duplicated as necessary.

However, as fuel became more plentiful, the restrictions on private motoring were eased, encouraging a steady increase in the number of cars on the road. Wages started to increase during the war and this had the effect of not only raising operating costs for bus companies, but also people began to enjoy better standards of living with more disposable income, making it easier to save for high-value items such as cars. Once available regularly, the car meant that few would wish to return to regular bus travel. Higher wages and more costly materials inevitably led to the need for economies, especially regarding manning levels, and applications were made to the Licensing Authority for fare increases. Thus, what we know today as inflation began to take hold and the stage was set for initial consolidation and then decline in H&C and also in many other rural bus operators throughout the country.

However, little of this was apparent in 1946, as the victory celebrations receded into memory and more men and women returned from the armed forces. New buses were still unavailable, even if they had been ordered speculatively during the war. Hutchings &

Hutchings & Cornelius' first new post-war vehicle was this Bedford OB with Mulliner bodywork delivered in March 1948. Prior to this early-1960s view at the St James Street depot in South Petherton, the bodywork had been partially rebuilt at Vincents Yeovil workshops. (Author's collection)

Cornelius obtained a Dennis Lancet with centre-entrance bodywork by D.J. Davies from the R.A.F. Registered ANY 500, it became the first vehicle to carry a new standard livery of light blue with grey lining, which replaced the cream and black colour scheme. Some buses had also been carrying a livery described as green and brown.

Purchased from the Ministry of Supply in June 1946 and kept at Barrington was an Austin utility 10 cwt van registered GYD 124 which was used as a support vehicle. In 1947 came two second-hand Bedford OWB utility buses, similar to those acquired previously. These permitted the withdrawal of some worn-out elderly vehicles.

In September 1946, the directors were considering a new bus service from Yeovil to new housing at Larkhill Road, north of Preston Plucknett. Joint operation with Southern National was proposed. In the event, it was the latter company which started a service, numbered 1B.

From 28 April 1947, the service to Taunton via Isle Brewers was diverted to serve the village of Isle Abbots, between Fivehead and Curry Mallet. In that November, an application was made to extend the Yeovil–West Chinnock service through to Crewkerne on weekdays except Thursdays, following a request from the local council, and this started on 16 February 1948. In April 1948, application was made for a separate licence for the works service to the Westland Factory from South Petherton, Norton, Stoke and Montacute, following which the factory was no longer served by a detour on certain journeys running into Yeovil.

The management of H&C discouraged union activities, but by 1947 certain members of staff were becoming interested in proper representation owing to the low rates of pay, especially for long 'spreadover' shifts which started at 9 a.m. and finished at 11 p.m., including breaks of up to four hours for which no pay was received. Matters reached a

A rare Seddon Mark IV with Perkins engine and Associated Coachbuilders body, KYD 379 was purchased from a Taunton dealer in April 1949. Delivered in the recently introduced blue and grey livery, it was sold for scrap after only thirteen years service. The location is Crown Lane, South Petherton, near the garage. (J. Fielder/R. Marshall collection)

head in May and there was a short strike. Several of the staff held a secret meeting in the yard of the Wyndham Arms at Kingsbury Episcopi, where driver Jack Bindon was the licensee, and they were addressed by a union representative. A wage award was forthcoming and this, coupled with poor passenger-carrying in January and February due to the extremely hard weather, meant that the company's net profit level in 1947 was of some concern to the directors.

In March 1948, H&C took delivery of a thirty-one-seat Bedford OB bus with attractive bodywork by Mulliner, registered JYC 426, this being the first new post-war vehicle. This was joined by a similar machine in November 1949, registered LYC 10. Also purchased new in this period was KYA 238, a Lee-bodied Dennis Lancet J3 coach. The chassis of this vehicle was ordered for October 1946, but the preferred body-builder – Duple – was unable to take any new orders, with little prospect of delivery until 1949! Eventually, Lee Motors completed its body by July 1948. KYD 379 was a twenty-nine-seat Seddon coach fitted with a Perkins engine, bought from a dealer in Taunton, and LYC 129 a twenty-seven-seat Austin with Reading bodywork. Coaches were suitable for use on bus or contract work when required.

With petrol still in short supply, H&C considered disposing of their Standard car, previously used for taxi work, which had been off the road since the end of 1948 as the petrol ration was considered insufficient. In July 1949, Ernie Cartwright announced that he would stand down as a director of H&C and transfer his shares to Alf Cornelius' sons, but this did not occur at that time.

Langport, on the H&C South Petherton–Taunton service in October 1963 is the setting for this view of Austin CXB LYC 129, with bodywork by Readings of Portsmouth. It spent fifteen years with H&C from 1950. (R. Lee)

Summer 1950 saw the arrival of two very unusual buses. Registered MYA 391 and 816, they were forty-seat Jensens with bodies by Sparshatts, both relatively rare on Public Service Vehicles. These were full-fronted with the passenger entrance forward of the front wheel arch, with the Perkins engine mounted vertically between the driver's compartment and the entrance. They were the largest capacity single-deckers to operate in the area and when the first one was parked in The Square at South Petherton, it attracted considerable attention from the locals. MYA 391 had been a demonstration model, and negotiations for its purchase were carried out at Barrington. The deal was done after Alf Cornelius had suggested the installation of some additional fittings to make it acceptable to him.

In March 1951 an application was made to extend the service licensed to run between South Petherton and Barrington only, through to Ilminster via Puckington and Stocklinch. One journey each way double-ran to Westport *en route*, and the extension started by the summer of that year. At the same time, a Sunday service was introduced on the South Petherton–Taunton service, although it appears that this, and the Westport diversion mentioned above were unsuccessful and were withdrawn again in spring 1957.

The last vehicle purchased under Cornelius auspices was also a radical departure. This was a double-decker which went into service on the South Petherton–Yeovil service on 17 July 1953. Purchased from Don Everall, the Wolverhampton dealer, it had originally come from the Huddersfield Corporation fleet and was a Daimler CWA6 with a fifty-five-seat lowbridge body (with sunken upper-deck gangway) built by Brush of Loughborough. It was very useful on the busier Yeovil journeys and probably saved the use of a 'duplicate' vehicle at peak times.

And now for something completely different – a rare and unusual type of bus which looked very advanced for its time when delivered in summer 1950. MYA 391 was a Jensen with its lightweight Sparshatts body containing forty seats – a high capacity at that time. Although the driver sat in line with the passenger entrance, the cab could only be accessed from a door on the off-side. (R. Marshall collection)

In an effort to economise on the amount of 'relief' buses and crews needed on the popular South Petherton–Yeovil service, H&C acquired in 1953 CCX 660, a wartime utility Daimler CWA6 double-decker with a Brush fifty-five-seat lowbridge body. Originally in the municipal Huddersfield fleet, it is laying over in South Petherton in July 1957, shortly before withdrawal. (R. Lee)

The first vehicle to arrive after Vincents gained full control of H&C from the Cornelius family was RYD 143 in June 1954. It was an Austin CXD with centre-entrance thirty-two-seat bodywork by Strachan of Hamble, Hants. It was scrapped after an accident near Yeovil in December 1963. (R. Marshall collection)

Perhaps hearing of Alf Cornelius' intentions, the board of Southern National made an offer of £42,000 for the H&C business in 1953, but this appears to have been withdrawn at the last minute. So when Cornelius retired in spring 1954, he sold his shareholding to the Vincent family who thus took full control of H&C and retained the company entity. Stanley Vincent became chairman and his sons John and Paul were made directors. Strategic decisions were henceforth made at Vincents' Yeovil office, and Fred Alford stayed on as manager at South Petherton while Len Cornelius supervised operations at Barrington on a day-to-day basis. Alf Cornelius continued to live at Cornhill House, having left the Royal Oak at Barrington during the war.

The first new vehicles purchased under Vincent control came in June 1954. RYD 143 was a thirty-two-seat centre-entrance Austin CXD coach with Strachan body while RYD 144 was a forty-four-seat service bus by the same bodybuilder but on a Dennis Lancet UF LU2 chassis. 'UF' stood for underfloor engine, the first of the type in the H&C fleet. This would have been quite a novelty in the area and when RYD 144 was new, driver Howard Drayton took the village bell-ringers on a day trip to Exeter in it. With these two vehicles came a new standard livery of red and cream, and older vehicles were also gradually repainted into these colours. Two further Dennis Lancet UF came in April 1955, with forty-one-seat front-entrance, dual-purpose Strachan Everest bodywork.

Not long after, it was recognised that the chassis of Dennis Lancets CUP 282 and KYA 238 were acceptable but the bodies were showing signs of wear. They were therefore refurbished and given new bodies by Vincents in their Yeovil workshops, which were full-fronted with bus seats inside. Perhaps this was an indication that it was no longer viable to buy new vehicles as replacements every time. Subsequently, Vincents re-bodied Bedford

The first underfloor-engined bus with H&C and the most modern looking to date was RYD 144, a Dennis Lancet LU2 of June 1954. The somewhat austere bodywork was by Strachan. During the 1950s, H&C was to remain loyal to Dennis for their full-size vehicle intake. (R. Marshall collection)

The next pair of Dennis Lancet LU2s arrived in April 1955, at which point Bedford OWB FYD 138 and Dennis Arrow Minor CYC 422 were withdrawn. They carried Strachan Everest forty-one-seat dual-purpose bodies. TYC 319 is seen here at Exmouth on coach duties in June 1962. (R. Partridge)

Hutchings & Cornelius' next new vehicles were three underfloor-engined Lancets with Harrington bodies, in 1957. The first, YYB 117 is parked at Taunton awaiting its next journey, alongside similar 632 CYB of 1958. (R. Marshall)

OWB FYD 137 – this retained its petrol engine but got new seats which had been taken out of Austin LYC 129, after the latter had gained improved coach seating. Partial body rebuilds were carried out on the two Bedford OB buses and these gained Perkins diesel engines, giving them a few more years of life at a reasonable cost.

In 1957 during the Suez Crisis, when there were severe concerns about fuel supplies, the Government looked to bus operators for a 10 per cent reduction in mileage operated in order to help conserve stocks. As a result, H&C reduced the number of journeys on the Taunton via Isle Brewers service and withdrew the Ilminster–Barrington–Yeovil service on Tuesdays, when demand may have decreased to point where it was no longer economic to run it. The fuel situation could also have had a bearing on the decision to withdraw the South Petherton–Taunton service on Sundays, mentioned earlier.

A second Daimler CWA6 double-decker arrived in April 1957, from Trent Motor Traction, registered RC 8482 and this ran alongside the first one until the latter was withdrawn five months later. Three more new Dennis Lancet UF vehicles came in summer 1957, this time with Harrington bodies, registered YYB117/118/119, being suitable for both bus and coach work. Hutchings & Cornelius were the first company in the area to introduce 'one man operation', whereby the driver collects the fares and issues tickets – a practice that it is now almost universal. Until the late 1940s, H&C conductors used Bell Punch tickets, which were pre-printed with a fare value and were carried in a hand-held rack, and then cancelled by a small punch machine. These were replaced by the Bellgraphic ticket system, whereby a ticket roll runs past an aperture in the top of the

Dennis Lancet J3 KYA 238, new in 1948, had its original Lee body removed and replaced by a new one built by Vincents, in an attempt to portray a more modern image instead of the half-cab layout, which was becoming rapidly unfashionable. It looks like washday in Yeovil. (R. Marshall)

A remarkably unusual purchase for a small country bus operator was East Lancs-bodied Dennis Loline 1 623 BYA. This fleet flagship performed on the SouthPetherton/Crewkerne –Yeovil services and replaced Daimler RC 8482 in 1958. The painted advertising between the decks ensured that H&C's owners got permanent promotion of their Austin car dealership. In 1973, the Loline was the last conductor-operated bus. (Author's collection)

The Loline double-decker was the largest bus in the fleet. Then came the smallest! 708 BYB was an Austin J2 eleven-seater, with body converted to PSV standard by Kenex. Comfort was best described as 'basic', but it was only intended for relatively short journeys, such as those made by darts teams to local pubs or bringing in people from the villages to join an excursion coach. (R. Marshall collection)

122 BYD was a similar Austin J2 to that shown in the previous photograph, although with a larger area of dark red paintwork. It is parked in the St James Street yard at South Petherton in 1963. (R. Marshall)

machine and the fare value is written in by the conductor with a pencil, before the ticket is torn off.

A new 'pride of the fleet' was delivered in June 1958 to replace the old Daimler double-decker. This was 623 BYA a Dennis Loline 1 with a sixty-eight-seat East Lancs body, featuring powered doors on the rear platform. It had a Gardner engine and at that time was the largest capacity vehicle in the Western Traffic Area. It was similar to a batch of vehicles then being purchased by the Aldershot & District Traction Co., and was a singular choice for a small independent operator running rural services.

The year 1958 also saw the arrival of two eleven-seat Austin J2 minibuses, which were bought for use on a school contract and also for small-party private hire, such as darts teams. They had two entrances – a sliding door at the side and a conventional pair at the back, and they were painted grey and maroon. The conversion of the British Motor Corporation bodies to Public Service Vehicle standard was undertaken by Kenex, and they were known as 'Kenecoaches'. To round off the year, the last Dennis Lancet UF arrived, registered 632 CYB, again with Harrington bodywork. Meanwhile, the last half-cab vehicle, Dennis Lancet BTE 861 was withdrawn.

six
The way it was

Although all bus operators hopefully aspire to provide a good level of service to their customers, that given by H&C was remarkable, with a strong community focus. It was people who gave the company its special identity, involving some real characters among both the staff and the passengers. Perhaps it is time to pause to move away from factual developments and relate a miscellany of memories and anecdotes as recalled by former staff and those who used the services. These are recorded as described to the author.

Country bus operation in Somerset in days gone by was sometimes less formalised than today. Driver Fred Virgin liked cider. He would do the early run from South Petherton and on reaching Pen Mill, the landlord of the Great Western Hotel would let him in for a pint of cider and a sandwich. Back at South Petherton, he would go into the Crown for a repeat of the same and so on for the rest of his shift.

One of the pair of 1943 utility Bedford OWBs had its body rebuilt by Vincents which gave it an extended life, and its appearance offers a comparison with the earlier photograph of FYD 138. It is seen here waiting for the children outside Kingsbury Episcopi school at Stembridge in June 1967, five months before withdrawal, prior to setting off for Barrington. (R. Lee)

The second Jensen of the pair was MYA 816 which, like its twin, lasted until 1964. Note the stencilled cut-out letters 'JNSN' over the radiator, an abbreviation of course for Jensen. They had Perkins engines. (Author's collection)

Like JYD 426, the second Bedford OB was rebuilt in later life by Vincents, hence the relatively modern side windows. Withdrawn in early 1963, it waits at the Taunton terminus. The Bedford petrol engines were replaced by Perkins diesel units. (R. Jenkins/R. Marshall collection)

Another driver was Herbie Meade, to whom time appeared to mean little. He rarely exceeded 30mph and being keen on taking snuff, he would stop his bus to have a chat with anybody he knew who also took it, and to exchange a pinch. Herbie used to wear cycle clips when driving, to prevent the wind whistling up his legs from around the brake and clutch pedals.

Dennis Single, who was a mechanic for H&C from 1946 to 1960, having worked for Vincents in Yeovil before the war, was driving one of the small pre-war Dennis buses back from Yeovil to Barrington when the clutch failed. Not wanting to inconvenience or delay his passengers, he changed gear without using the clutch. He managed to nurse the bus back to Barrington in a somewhat jumpy fashion, slowing down to a crawl so that people could alight without the bus having to come to a halt. At Barrington he parked the bus in the street and went into the garage to get a replacement vehicle, on which he took the passengers for Stocklinch and Ilminster. Dennis thought he had done quite well, until one elderly man alighting commented that in his view, he thought Dennis had made a 'far better hash of driving the second bus than the first', obviously oblivious to the previous problem.

As well as passengers, H&C carried large quantities of parcels and other goods from their suppliers to the customers, especially where the traders did not carry out local deliveries or when fuel was on ration. Indeed, H&C carried everything from newspapers to plants from a nursery. For example, in 1937 the parcel agent in Taunton was despatching an average of thirty packages a day and on one occasion the total was sixty! This was Harry Clark's hairdresser's shop at Elms Parade, opposite the H&C terminus point.

Conductress Edna Dinham, who worked for H&C in the late 1940s, recalls that people in South Petherton used to order meat pies from Norman Hawkins' bakery in Shepton

On stage-carriage duties at Yeovil is TYC 320, the other 1955 Dennis Lancet LU2. Both it and TYC 319 were withdrawn in the late 1960s. (Author's collection)

Beauchamp and once a week they were sent on the bus in a box, and left at Fred Hallett's barber's shop next to Cornhill House in The Square for collection by customers. Apparently, Norman used the same box for a number of years! On Thursdays, fish would be regularly sent by bus from Taunton to the fishmonger at Curry Rivel, no doubt to the chagrin of the passengers and crew.

Rural bus services often emulated their forerunner – the Carrier, in terms of the range of commodities which were carried. Drivers and conductors were expected to deal with all that came their way, such as delivering papers and other items to people's doors at isolated houses along the routes. Some of the more unusual items that found their way onto H&C buses included brass plates for coffins, which were sent to Taunton for engraving by Cyril Clark, the Barrington undertaker, and various samples and specimens sent by village doctors for collection at the terminus by laboratory staff for analysis. Car parts including bulky exhaust pipes were taken from Taunton to Bill Paul's garage at Westport. And just for good measure, one conductor would have to sell the popular weekly tickets on Monday morning on the three buses which were needed on the early journey from South Petherton to Taunton.

Quite a few people in the villages would be 'outworkers', making components at home for various garments. Alf Cornelius' wife Emily would stitch shirt collars, which were then put on the bus for collection by Van Heusens in Taunton, while others used the buses for the despatch of 'gloving'.

The buses were also important for local inter-village journeys. People from Barrington would catch the 12.10 p.m. bus to Shepton Beauchamp so as to get their bread from Hawkins' bakery, with just enough time to return on the 12.45 p.m. In the evening, residents of these villages would use H&C to get to and from the pub. The bus could never depart until everyone had been extracted from the bar!

A second lowbridge Daimler CWA6 double-decker, RC 8482 with Duple body was purchased in April 1957, having been in the fleet of Trent Motor Traction. It is in H&C's Vicarage Street bus park in Yeovil, flanked by Dennis Lancet RYD 144 and Jensen MYA 816. (R. Marshall)

Dennis Lancet YYB 118 waits at Yeovil, ready for its return journey to Barrington via Kingsbury Episcopi, the Lambrooks and Shepton Beauchamp. (R. Marshall)

In the late 1950s, Vincents put a new body onto CUP 282, a wartime Dennis Lancet purchase. It makes an interesting contrast with the underfloor-engined Lancet variant, YYB 118 at Taunton. Compare the appearance of CUP 282 with its earlier photograph. (J. Parke/Omnibus Society)

Hutchings & Cornelius staff always knew what to expect from the regular passengers. For example, if the crew saw latecomers running down from Rock Hill to the main road near Wrantage, they would not dream of departing until they were all safely on the bus. If the Taunton bus was full by the time it reached Wrantage, the driver would signal over his shoulder to indicate that a relief vehicle was behind and that there was no need for panic.

John Cornelius recalls that in the mid-1950s a young lady from the hamlet of Swell would walk three-quarters of a mile down to the main road between Fivehead and Curry Rivel to catch the bus to work in Taunton. One morning, she was not there when the bus arrived. Driver Fred Morris stopped and advised his passengers that they had better wait for her as the next bus was not until 10a.m. Sure enough, a few minutes later she came running down the road, quite relieved that she had not missed the bus and half a day's pay. Yet that was the way H&C looked after their regulars and why they preferred H&C to National.

It was not only big cities like London which suffered from the very heavy fogs or 'smog' in the winters of the late 1940s/early 1950s, when most houses were heated by coal fires. Conductress Joan Smith recalls leaving Taunton at 6 p.m. for South Petherton and having to walk in front of the bus at Henlade so as to guide driver Herbie Meade.

One day Fred Welch and Johnny Brake drove two coaches on an excursion to Weymouth. On the way into the town, they found themselves in a traffic queue. Quite a few people had gathered around two cars. The front bumper of one had ridden up over the rear bumper of the other and nobody seemed to know the best way of releasing them. Johnny, being a big strong man, eyed up the situation and said 'stand back', then physically lifted the offending car clear, much to the relief of the vehicle owners and the other motorists who could then be on their way.

Dennis Lancet YYB 119 is at Taunton. The trio of 1957 Lancets was in extensive use on bus services until the early 1970s, with this one being sold to a preservation group in Guildford in Surrey. (Author's collection)

Two neat little H&C Albion Nimbuses await their next journeys at Yeovil. This lightweight type of rural bus had a tendency to slide around in icy road conditions. (R. Marshall)

Somewhat elderly by the time of purchase by H&C in 1967 is this 1953 Bedford SB (petrol engine) with Duple bodywork, but it only stayed in the fleet for just over two years. (R. Lee)

A resident of South Petherton has recalled her daily journey to Ilminster Grammar School by H&C bus during the war. The children called it the Hot & Cold bus – it was sometimes hot on board but more often cold! The buses were heavily loaded and the rear of the vehicle would touch the road if it went over a bump or a humped-back bridge.

In the late 1940s, the peak-hour Taunton journeys were so heavily laden with standing passengers that the bus mudguards would scrape on the road at the sharp corner near Thornfalcon school. During the era of national service, it was not unknown for there to be more than 100 servicemen on board one of the forty-seat Jensen buses for the trip back from Yeovil.

During the period of food rationing, there was a lady from Barrington who caught the bus every Friday, so she could get a cheese sandwich from Woolworths in Taunton – luxury indeed! Hutchings & Cornelius staff were often favoured with 'a little bit extra' on their ration by some of the shopkeepers for whom they delivered goods by bus.

Fifty years ago, a coach driver had to work much harder than today. There was a steep hill near Crewkerne called Winyard's Gap, where the radiators of coaches on excursions to the coast would boil. The drivers would often have to stop to top them up from a specially-positioned water butt. In winter at South Petherton, the somewhat risky technique of using a blow lamp to unfreeze a petrol engine was supplemented by a local person who would tow the buses with an old army jeep, and he apparently burnt out at least one clutch by so doing.

Alf Cornelius was always proud that he painted the buses by hand himself. He was painting one in the road outside the garage at Barrington, and then went for lunch. He met a commercial traveller to whom he boasted 'I do all my own painting'. Imagine the effect on his pride and ego when he took the man outside to admire his handiwork, only

AEC Reliance/Willowbrook TYD 122G is in Yeovil Bus Station in April 1969, about a month after delivery. It carries the newly-introduced dark maroon and cream bus livery and the new-style H&C fleet name representation. (E. Shirras)

to discover that the black band which was painted on the cream background had run down the side of the bus in streaks.

Cyril Thorne recalled an incident involving a pre-war Dennis twenty-seat bus, known to the staff as 'Betsy'. George Gentle got it ready for Dick Osborne to use on a contract journey, and left it with the engine running outside of the garage at South Petherton, and told Dick it was there. The first George knew about something being wrong was when Dick went back into the garage, and said 'It's not there!'. Both of them went outside and looked up and down and sure enough, there was 'Betsy' some way down Crown Lane, having come to rest against a wall, without serious damage, and with the engine still ticking over. George was so traumatised that he could not speak, but made a sort of stammering, gurgling noise.

Finally, it should be mentioned that regular H&C customers were very appreciative of the excellent service given by the staff. A Mrs Bird often used the Taunton route, and at Christmas she would present each driver and conductor with half a crown and a sponge cake. One can only wonder what the bus driver of today would make of such a gift. Happy days!

Displaying a 'Last Bus to South Petherton' notice is NYD 440L, the second Bristol LH with Leyland 401 engine. The location is the picturesque village of Drayton, on the main Taunton service, on 31 May 1979. The driver was a senior member of staff – Howard Drayton, by coincidence. (J. Cornelius)

seven
The 1960s

In January 1960, H&C ceased to use the yard in Crown Lane, South Petherton and transferred their parking area to a site at the south-east end of St James Street on the corner of Prigg Lane. This had a small garage building capable of holding two vehicles. Adjacent was the Territorial Army Hall, with the Conservative Club above it. During the 1920s, Fred Parsons had a garage business there with petrol pumps, while Messrs Walter & Parsons had a thirteen-seat Reo 27hp vehicle registered YA 9376 in 1924, and ran advertised excursions and private hire. Another local coach operator, Ernie Giles, also kept his vehicles there at times, and he will be encountered later, in the Safeway story. By 1960, the site was owned by the Vincent empire and could thus be conveniently leased to their H&C interest.

In June 1961 an AEC Reliance with thirty-seven-seat Harrington coach body introduced another chassis make into the fleet, as Dennis no longer produced single-deckers. This was allocated to Barrington depot as the principal private-hire and tours coach.

To assist in the replacement of small capacity buses, another unusual type of vehicle was chosen by H&C. In April 1962 they took delivery of two thirty-one-seat Albion Nimbus vehicles with bodywork by Harrington, the supplier then in vogue with the Vincent family. A similar machine came in January 1963 to replace LYC 10, the last Bedford OB. It was thus something of a surprise when Bedford OWB FYD 137 was again fully overhauled for further service the same year, lasting until 1967.

On 4 December 1963, Austin coach RYD 143 was written off in an accident on the West Coker Road at Yeovil. A driving instructor on his way to work was taken to hospital when his car went out of control and collided with the coach, which mounted the bank at the side of the road and toppled over. Also injured were H&C's driver and conductor, Ian Holmes and Bill Taylor. RYD 143 was sold to Mr Coles, a scrap dealer at Barwick near Yeovil, who also bought various other redundant H&C vehicles subsequently. Also in December 1963, 217 UYC was delivered, being another AEC Reliance, this time with a forty-five-seat Harrington bus body, which was the first in the fleet with air brakes.

On 3 February 1964, the Taunton terminus used since the early days at a parking area outside the Kings Arms Hotel in Elms Parade, was abandoned in favour of the Belvedere Road car park, which was some way from the town centre.

216 UYC, an AEC Reliance with a forty-one-seat Harrington Cavalier body, came in March 1964. It should have been delivered at the same time as the previous AEC but was returned to the manufacturers for rectification.

The train service between Taunton and Yeovil via Langport West, Martock and Montacute was withdrawn from 15 June 1964, as part of the programme of line closures suggested in the Beeching Report. There was little use made of it by people in Montacute, but H&C might have then picked up a little extra trade. However, it was

In 1961, with Dennis single-deckers no longer available, H&C switched their allegiance to AEC. 823 KYD was the first of twelve Reliances to Vincents order, carrying a Harrington body, primarily for private hire and excursion work. (R. Marshall collection)

An ideal size for the abundant local narrow lanes were three Albion Nimbuses with thirty-one-seat Harrington bodies – two arrived in April 1962 and a third in January 1963. 933 NYB waits at Taunton on 13 October 1962 to perform a 'back roads' journey to Isle Brewers. (R. Lee)

Western and Southern National who provided a 'rail replacement service', numbered 200 from Taunton to Yeovil via Langport, Kingsbury Episcopi, Martock, Stoke and Montacute, although it was infrequent and had local picking-up restrictions to protect H&C.

The new coaches in 1965 were further AEC/Harrington vehicles, this time of the latter's Grenadier model. Coach numbered BYD 735C was the first in the fleet with forced-air interior ventilation, while CYD 724C replaced 835 KYD at Barrington. In December 1965, Austin LYC 129 was sold to Vincent Finance Co.(Yeovil) Ltd, another part of H&C's owning group; they then hired it to British Railways for staff transport.

The local press announced in March 1966 that Yeovil Rural Council had granted planning permission to Vincents to redevelop the St James Street site in South Petherton. They envisaged a car showroom, petrol filling station, twelve lock-up garages and a public car park, but nothing transpired at that time. In October that year, timetable changes were made to bus services run from Barrington depot, including the withdrawal of the Ilminster–Barrington–Yeovil service on Mondays. Also, many of the journeys on the South Petherton–Yeovil service became one-man operated.

The first Dennis UF to be withdrawn was RYD 144 in March 1967, and it was kept to provide spare parts for the similar vehicles. A somewhat surprising second-hand purchase in June 1967 was an elderly petrol-engined Bedford SB coach with a Duple body, previously with a firm in Devon, but it only lasted just over two years with H&C.

On 22 May 1968, the new bus station in Yeovil opened for business. Sited on the corner of Central Road and Earle Street, it was served by all the H&C Yeovil services, of which the one to Ilminster was altered to terminate there rather than in Town Station Road. By September of that year, the Barrington to Ilminster section of the South Petherton–Ilminster service was reduced to run on Wednesday, Friday and Saturday only.

Seemingly fresh from the Harrington factory is Albion Nimbus 934 NYB, displaying a trade registration plate in the windscreen, possibly to allow a test run or delivery to Somerset. (Author's collection)

Harrington supplied the body on AEC Reliance 217 UYC, seen leaving Yeovil Bus Station in probably 1972, as it carries the later style of H53. Hutchings & Cornelius' fleet name can be seen on the side; behind it is a Western National Bristol LS. (R. Marshall)

The new coach in 1964 was 216 UYC, an AEC Reliance with attractive Harrington Grenadier forty-one-seat coachwork. Photographed at South Petherton in May 1965, it was sold in 1970 for further service with another well-known Somerset operator – Wakes of Sparkford. (R. Lee)

Possibly the ultimately aesthetically pleasing Harrington coach was the Grenadier model, a development of the previous Cavalier. Delivered in April 1965, this AEC Reliance was H&C's largest coach up to that time, and is seen residing at South Petherton depot. (Author's collection)

The last Harrington-bodied acquisition was forty-one-seat AEC Reliance CYD 724C of 1965, seen here on a private hire at Lydney in Gloucestershire. The driver is Stewart Jacobs. (J. Cornelius)

The last new vehicles of the decade were again AEC Reliances. Four had forty-five-seat Willowbrook bus bodies of a general style much used by some of the larger operators, featuring an attractive curved-front windscreen. The first one, TYC 250G was delivered in late November 1968 and introduced another new bus livery of cream above the waistline, and very dark maroon (some would say brown) below. A new style of fleet name was used, while the interior was illuminated by fluorescent strip lighting. These vehicles meant that H&C was now even more portraying a 'big company' image with its fleet. Another new AEC Reliance was a forty-one-seat coach with a Panorama Elite body by Plaxton.

By the 1960s, H&C had built up quite a programme of day and half-day coach excursions, starting from South Petherton but also calling at many of the surrounding villages on the H&C bus services. If a village was not on a convenient route for the destination, and there were people booked, they would be taken by a minibus to South Petherton to connect with the coach. Seats could be booked at Cornhill House and Barrington depot, as well as various individuals appointed as agents in the villages. In former years, there were special shuttle services to events like Yeovil Show, Ilminster Show and Bridgwater Fair. One year, the latter two events coincided and all available drivers worked very long hours to cope with the demand. For some years, H&C undertook the team transport for Yeovil Football Club.

When Barlow, Phillips & Co. of Yeovil gave up in 1960, their tours licence was offered to H&C but the price was more than they were prepared to pay. It passed to Darch and Willcox Ltd of Martock, who then applied to run their tours within a ten-mile radius of Martock, overlapping H&C territory. Ernie Giles, H&C and National all objected and the application was refused at the hearing.

Home-to-school transport contracts, usually for Somerset County Council, were performed by H&C for many years. In the late 1960s, they operated to Milford School in Yeovil from Mudford, to Preston Secondary School from Barwick and Stoford, to Stanchester Secondary School in Stoke Sub Hamden from South Petherton and Martock and to Kingsbury Episcopi School in Stembridge from Barrington, the Lambrooks and Kingsbury. Also, as well as the established works journeys to the Westlands factory, there was a contract to Rendall's Nurseries at Ilton from Shepton Beauchamp, Barrington, Westport and Puckington. This carried workers and also ran on Saturdays. It was started in the mid-1930s and at one time was driven by the fitter at Barrington depot, who kept a vehicle overnight in Ilminster for the purpose.

A new era of modernity was heralded in 1969 by four AEC Reliance forty-five-seat buses with Willowbrook bodies, of a similar design to any vehicles in the fleets of major operators. Two days before the end of H&C in 1979, TYC 250G pauses outside the Royal Oak at Barrington *en route* from Taunton to South Petherton. The bus garage in the background had closed nine years earlier. (J. Cornelius)

VYA 834G of 1969 was an AEC Reliance/Plaxton Panorama Elite coach. On one side is what appears to be demolition rubble cleared when the hard-standing was extended, and on the other is Dennis Lancet YYB 118, the longest survivor of that type. The coach carries the carnation red and ermine white livery. (Author's collection)

Another AEC/Willowbrook, WYD 928H, on 25 May 1979 at the latter-day H&C Taunton
terminus of Belvedere Road car park. It passed to Brutonian and continued to appear on rural bus
services across Dorset and Somerset for some while. (J. Cornelius)

eight
Difficult times

The swinging Sixties was a decade that built upon the second half of the 1950s as a period of immense socio-economic change. Shorter working hours, more wages and more employment opportunities resulted in a better way of life and more disposable income. Many were now leaving the traditional jobs and crafts of the countryside and heading for industrial estates in the towns, while better education encouraged some to move away from rural areas where their families had lived for generations, to seek opportunities in the wider world. It became almost standard for young people to take their driving test at the earliest opportunity and then buy a car, even if it was only a 'banger'. This did not bode well for the fortunes of the bus industry which in time found itself on the receiving end of assumptions such as 'only children, old people and those with no other choice use buses'. Also, the growth in ownership of telephones discouraged some travel for social visits while television had a profound effect on cinema and theatre patronage.

Less revenue for bus operators meant fewer buses and less frequent services, especially in the evening, on Sundays and in rural areas. The Government of the day recognised that this could cause problems and the Transport Act 1968 gave local authorities the power to offer subsidies or 'Revenue Support Grant' to assist operators in maintaining unremunerative services, although in reality the process was lengthy and sometimes when the money did come, it was too little too late. Subsequently, operators could receive a grant of up to 50 per cent of the cost of new vehicles, as long as they performed a stipulated part of their annual mileage on stage-carriage services. For most rural independent operators, a new vehicle was a novel experience, but of course H&C had always had them when possible. They were still to provide some surprises with their choice of vehicles but now specified them for either bus or coach work, rather than using those designed for various types of job. To promote the separation of the coach fleet, a new livery of carnation red and ermine white was chosen for them.

By 1970, operators of all sizes were significantly reducing their rural networks, to match the availability of Revenue Support Grant. Hutchings & Cornelius were finding it much harder to make ends meet and with the continuing regular intake of new vehicles, it is tempting to speculate whether Vincents were cross-subsidising H&C from their other activities. Fred Alford retired and Stanley Baker was appointed manager. He was a long-serving member of Vincents staff who had already been involved with H&C and he formulated a strategy to achieve cost savings. From 1 January 1970, the Crewkerne–Yeovil service was truncated to terminate at Yeovil Bus Station, rather than at Pen Mill, although this point continued to be the terminus for the South Petherton service.

In April 1970, H&C gave notice to the Traffic Commissioner that they would withdraw several services when the licences expired on 30 June. They were

In 1970, Fred Alford is presented with a retirement gift by Len Cornelius. Amongst the others in the picture are Charlie Cornelius, Gladys Alford, Jack Bindon, Ella Lock, Stan Harwood, Howard Drayton, Herbie Meade, Bernard Welch, Fred Virgin, Ned Best, Stanley Baker, Sam Blackwell, Joe Wrenn and Malcolm Neville. (Mrs M. Baker collection)

Plaxton Derwent bodywork was chosen for the 1970 AEC Reliance bus. CYA 181J, driven by Charlie Cornelius, sets off for Yeovil along St James Street in South Petherton on the last day, 31 May 1979. The name Cornelius is quite common in south Somerset as evidenced by the name on the shop in the background, and by the photographer. (J. Cornelius)

Ilminster–Barrington–Yeovil, South Petherton–Barrington–Ilminster, Barrington–Curry Mallet–Taunton and South Petherton–Westlands Factory. The situation was reviewed by the County Rural Bus Services sub-committee, made up of members from the County Council and the Borough and District Councils. In the event, a very limited service was provided on the Barrington services to Ilminster and Yeovil, basically offering a Friday afternoon shopping facility into the two towns, but the other services did cease. The size of the fleet could be reduced and new schedules saved on drivers. Barrington depot was closed, with all vehicles being kept at South Petherton. The St James Street site was enlarged by demolition of various structures, with hard-standing being provided to accommodate more vehicles.

In December 1970, another new AEC Reliance bus was purchased, this time with a Plaxton Derwent body, registered CYA 181J, followed in 1972 by KYA 905K, the last new H&C Reliance, fitted with a fifty-one-seat Willowbrook Expressway 002 dual-purpose body. In January 1972, H&C again showed its penchant for the unusual when it took delivery of a Bristol LH6L with a forty-five-seat ECW bus body. For many years, the Bristol/ECW combination was used extensively and exclusively by the nationalised Tilling Group companies, which included Southern and Western National – that is why Dennis built the Loline double-decker under licence from Bristol for supply to other companies, it being a derivative of Bristol's famous Lodekka. Identical Bristol LHs were being delivered to the National companies in the West Country and elsewhere, and H&C's model, registered GYC 160K must have felt at home in Yeovil or Taunton. A year later, another one arrived, but with two fewer seats, and replaced a Dennis Lancet UF.

Hutchings & Cornelius still had one more surprise for the industry and the bus enthusiast when in June 1973 they took delivery of RYA 700L, a Bristol VRT double-decker with standard ECW seventy-seat body. This was the first Bristol

By purchasing two Bristol LHs with ECW bodywork in the early 1970s, H&C was emulating its long-time larger neighbour Western National, and other nationalised bus undertakings. GYC 160K is at Belvedere Road in Taunton when quite new in 1972. (D. Withers)

double-decker to be delivered to an independent operator, after the restriction on such sales was lifted, and replaced the Dennis Loline to achieve total one-man operation.

October 1973 heralded the start of H&C's Ford period. From then until December 1978, the Ford lightweight 'R' series vehicles found favour with the company on cost grounds as they were cheaper to buy and operate than, say, AECs or Leylands. There were seven coaches with either Plaxton or Duple bodywork, of which three were purchased new, including OYC 241P, the last such acquisition by H&C. While the coaches were acceptable for medium-distance private hire and local contracts, the two buses (one new, one second-hand) were less successful on the more arduous stage-carriage work.

Stanley Vincent died on 25 June 1975, leaving his sons John and Paul in control of the various family businesses, including H&C.

A cheap purchase for contract work in June 1976 was an elderly second-hand Bedford SB5 coach which lasted about seven months in the fleet, while in October that year came a rear-engined Leyland Atlantean double-decker from Glasgow, for a school contract where the number of pupils carried exceeded the capacity of a coach. An attractive fifty-one-seat AEC Reliance with a Willowbrook bus body was acquired from Safeguard of Guildford in September 1977. At this time, the fleet contained ten buses and six coaches, only CYD 724C (AEC/Harrington) and the Atlantean SGD 654 being built pre-1969.

In the mid-1970s, the Bellgraphic ticket machines were replaced by Setright machines, which printed the fare details on a narrow paper roll. As there were so few Bellgraphic machines then in use nationally, Bell Punch found it no longer viable to produce the ticket rolls.

Parcels traffic was still significant; some of the buses had boots which could often be quite full. Goddard & Son had nurseries at Lopen Head and dispatched their blooms in

Spending the day in Weymouth on 7 July 1974 is KYA 905K, the last AEC Reliance bought new by H&C. It carries the box-like Willowbrook Expressway body which was marketed for coach or dual-purpose work. (Author's collection)

H&C's second new double-decker was RYA 700L, maintaining the Bristol/ECW precedent set by the two LHs. This VRT model had a particularly smart appearance created by the livery and sign-writing. It is reversing away from the H&C departure point at Yeovil Bus Station in August 1975, when just over two years old. (M. Penn)

H&C's third Ford coach was EMB 167K, an R226 model with fifty-three-seat Plaxton Panorama Elite bodywork, purchased in September 1974 and coming from the large fleet of Shearings of Altrincham. It is parked outside the depot in South Petherton. (R. Lee)

long boxes to florists in Taunton and Yeovil. It was not unusual for there to be six or seven boxes, particularly on a Friday for a Saturday wedding. In contrast, another regular package was a bag of documents sent each day between the offices in South Petherton and Yeovil of Poole & Co., Solicitors.

In 1976, 400,000 passenger journeys were made on the main bus services. This compares with 784,000 on all services in 1949.

Returning now to the bus services, the company felt that it had the resources available to reintroduce one round trip on Saturdays from Westport into Taunton via Isle Brewers, Isle Abbots and Curry Mallet, allowing just over three hours for shopping. Started on 6 February 1971, it survived its three-month trial period, so patronage must have been satisfactory. In March 1971 the Sunday service was withdrawn from the South Petherton–Yeovil route. By 1976, only the odd journey on this service called at Houndstone Camp, but on 8 January, H&C started a round trip for shopping in Yeovil on Thursdays, from the married quarters at the camp. This was often worked by the Willowbrook Expressway-bodied AEC Reliance, having a large rear luggage locker which was useful for all the pushchairs.

For many years, Southern National had run their service 14 from Bower Hinton and Martock into Yeovil via Ash and Tintinhull, having consolidated their operations by the acquisition of the Wintle & Murray business. Some journeys reached South Petherton, primarily for bus and crew trips to and from their depot there, this service being renumbered 472 in 1969. However, there was no bus link from Martock to Taunton, and following a request from Martock Parish Council, H&C received dispensation from the Traffic Commissioner to do this from 3 October 1977. A short-term licence was issued so

JYB 538N was the Ford R1014/Plaxton Derwent bus bought new in April 1975. It was more typical of a small independent operator's bus than many of the vehicles owned by H&C, and after closure of the firm, it passed to Wimpey, the building contractor, for staff transport. (J. Cornelius)

that some journeys on the Taunton–South Petherton service could be extended to Hurst and Martock on Mondays to Saturdays, to ascertain which were the most suitable days of the week for the longer term. Eventually, it was decided that journeys to Martock should run on Wednesdays, Fridays and Saturdays, commencing 30 January 1978.

Over the years, there had been various attempts by H&C and National to co-ordinate the timetable between South Petherton and Yeovil, to avoid wasteful duplication, which resulted in there being a reasonable spacing between the journeys of the two companies. However, by the mid-1970s it was questionable if there was enough custom overall to warrant the number of journeys then being provided, as the financial climate in the bus industry was by then very different. Western National were receiving substantial Revenue Support from the County Council for their rural services in Somerset, and no doubt the Local Authority was keen to explore ways that operating costs and therefore funding could be reduced.

After competing on the South Petherton–Montacute–Yeovil route for so long, discussions between H&C, Western National and Somerset County Council resulted in an overall settlement between the companies with H&C becoming in sole charge from 22 May 1978.

Service 466 (renumbered from 6 in 1969) also served Lower Odcombe between Montacute and Preston. Hutchings & Cornelius consolidated the timings of their own journeys and those run by Western National on both the South Petherton and Crewkerne services to Yeovil, with most journeys diverting to Lower Odcombe as well as school time and Friday shopping journeys introduced from Higher Odcombe into Yeovil. The event was marked by the publication of a new timetable folder incorporating a brief history of

Looking somewhat dated when acquired for contract work in 1976, 995 OHW was a Bedford SB5 with Duple bodywork, previously owned by the well-known firm Wessex of Bristol. It was only in stock for about six months. (R. Lee)

The main purpose of acquiring this Leyland Atlantean double-decker from Glasgow in 1976 was to provide increased capacity on a school contract. Its distinctive Alexander bodywork was typical of large Scottish fleets, and was photographed at the Weymouth bus rally in July 1977. (Author's collection)

H&C, written and designed by Ray Stenning who in recent years has gone on to design the livery of buses and trains for many of today's major operators who are household names nationally.

The final service alteration was in autumn 1978 when a Thursday journey on the main Taunton service was diverted off the A378 road to double-run to Fivehead village, but this only lasted about six weeks as an experiment.

nine
The finale and afterwards

School contract requirements prompted H&C's last vehicle acquisition being another second-hand Leyland Atlantean, this time from Nottingham with a Metro Cammell body to the distinctive design of that municipality. This was DAU 427C which arrived in January 1979, replacing the earlier Atlantean and also a Ford coach.

H&C fares were always lower than the parallel National services and much was made of this by the local press when Western National service 466 was absorbed in 1978. However, this was not enough to halt declining patronage for the reasons outlined earlier, at a time of rising costs for fuel, insurance and spare parts for the vehicles. Vincents had probably been closely examining the continuing viability of H&C and possibly the catalyst in reaching their decision was a demand from certain of the drivers for a significant wage increase, stated by Vincents as being by 22 per cent, and that was beyond the company's means without raising fares which they felt would only further decrease patronage.

It had long been a grievance of drivers on the Yeovil services that although they worked as hard as their counterparts on Western National and carried more passengers, they got paid less. When H&C took over service 466, the drivers felt entitled to a wage award in view of the extra income for the company. The directors replied that they were unable to do this. The drivers wanted an increase, but did not seek the full T&GWU rates. However, they suggested that if the company was unwilling to comply, they would join the union and have their rates and conditions imposed. The directors' response was to close the company rather than to accede. The bus services were apparently ineligible for Revenue Support Grant from the County Council and it seems that Vincents did not approach the latter for financial assistance as they had already made their decision to close H&C.

On 19 March, Vincents made an announcement and John Vincent was quoted in the *Western Daily Press* next day as saying 'some of the drivers have been with us for forty years. We will be helping with redundancy payments and approaching other employers on their behalf'. He went on to say that the directors would like to place on record their thanks for the support of the staff but that they could see no future for the company. Naturally, there was widespread local anxiety among bus users and various local councillors who were quick to deplore the consequences of Vincents' decision but could do little that was tangible to prevent it. Some of the villagers of Kingsbury Episcopi met to discuss the matter and to consider whether to lobby for some kind of minibus service. Both Safeway Services and Western National showed cautious interest when the County Council sounded them out over taking over some of the services, but it would have been ironic if National had regained their service 466 which they had given up so recently.

In April, the AEC/Harrington coach was sold to nearby Taylors Coaches at Tintinhull, while AEC/Willowbrook bus FPC 15J moved home to the other end of South Petherton, being acquired by Safeway. Shortly afterwards, the news came that from Friday 1 June 1979 Safeway Services would take over the South Petherton/Crewkerne–Yeovil services, the Friday journeys from South Petherton to Ilminster and Ilminster to Yeovil, and the Thursday express bus to Yeovil from Houndstone Camp, together with a school contract to Crewkerne and the H&C Excursions and Tours licence.

Applications for the two Taunton services were made by both Western National and by Brutonian, a small independent company from Bruton owned by Chris Knubley. As the Traffic Commissioner was unable to arrange a public hearing until 18 June, Western National were instructed to run both services on a short-term basis using H&C's timetable and fares, without prejudice to the outcome.

The last day, 31 May 1979 saw H&C doing good business as many local people travelled for their last rides, supplemented by a number of bus enthusiasts from various parts of the country. It being a Thursday, the last H&C bus was due to arrive back at South Petherton from Yeovil around 10.15 p.m. The driver was Ken Harvey, and with champagne provided by the Vincent brothers, a carnival atmosphere prevailed. The bus was delayed by well-wishers at Montacute and Stoke, and a large crowd had gathered at the Prigg Lane parking area in South Petherton, when the bus finally arrived at 10.45 p.m., amid cheering and clapping. After 'three cheers for H&C', and the singing of *Auld Lang Syne*, everybody dispersed and H&C was no more, at least in the eyes of the public. Sixty-two-year-old Charlie Cornelius, having joined his father's business when he was fifteen, went to work for Safeway Services.

However, these events were not a source of jollification to everyone. Several drivers were not there to witness the last journeys, with natural bitterness for losing their jobs, for some after the best part of a lifetime's work. A rather acrimonious and sad end to a local institution, with a strong 'family' atmosphere among the staff.

The H&C company was retained by Vincents for 'fleet operation management consultancy services', and Stanley Baker was its last employee, continuing to work in Vincents' Yeovil office until his retirement.

As well as the services mentioned above, Safeway acquired three more buses from H&C – two of the forty-five-seat AEC Reliances with Willowbrook bodies and Bristol LH6L NYD 440L, as well as several members of staff and events which will be covered more later. As new licences had not been granted, Western National ran the Taunton services with 'On Hire to H&C' notices displayed on the vehicles and numbered the route from South Petherton as 263 and the Saturday-only service via Isle Brewers as 262. After a Traffic Court Hearing, Western National were granted the licence for service 263 from 2 July, with two extra buses being needed at their South Petherton depot, the total then being one Bristol LH and three Bristol RE single-deckers. The other service passed to Brutonian, who numbered it 15 and increased it to run on both Wednesdays and Saturdays. It was extended to start at South Petherton and then travel via Seavington St Michael, Whitelackington, Stocklinch and Puckington, to join the old H&C route at Westport. The Saturday service started on 7 July, and the Wednesday service on 25 July. To augment their fleet at that time, Brutonian acquired AEC Reliances WYD 928H and CYA 181J from H&C.

Today, First Somerset & Avon, as Southern National has become, runs services from Martock through Kingsbury Episcopi, South Petherton, Shepton Beauchamp, Barrington and Stocklinch into Ilminster and on to Taunton via Ilton and Hatch Beauchamp, also a Saturday journey into Taunton via Westport and Curry Rivel. These are supplemented by a Thursday service operated by Wakes from Yeovil to Taunton on a roundabout route

On the last day of operations, the depot yard was host to this pair of Duple Dominant-bodied Ford coaches. KYA 386N was bought new in June 1975 whilst JUN 199P on the right came from Loverings Coaches of Combe Martin in Devon.
(J. Cornelius)

Hailing from Scotland, having been with Newtons of Dingwall, was GST 423N, a Ford R1014 with Duple Dominant bus body. On 31 May 1979 it poses outside the garage in Crown Lane, South Petherton.
(J. Cornelius)

The last vehicle to be bought by H&C was DAU 427C, another Leyland Atlantean, this time with a Metro Cammell body to the design of its former owner, Nottingham City Transport. Seemingly soon after it arrived, it sits in the depot yard still in Nottingham green and cream livery. (R. Lee)

Above: John Cornelius caught this view of Dennis Winter, Malcolm Neville, Bert Down, Bernard Welch and Stan Harwood putting a brave face on what was a sad occasion, the end of an era spanning fifty-one years, and the passing of a public transport icon in south Somerset. (J. Cornelius)

Left: Long-serving driver Stan Harwood tries to look cheerful and stands in front of the Ford bus JYB 538N on the last day, 31 May 1979. (J. Cornelius)

In the last days of H&C, Howard Drayton, Charlie Cornelius and Jack Bindon stand in front of the Bristol VR. (G. Alford)

through Montacute, Bower Hinton, Martock, South Petherton, Barrington, Westport and Curry Rivel, while the needs of Isle Brewers and Curry Mallet are covered by a number of infrequent services into Langport, Taunton and Ilminster provided by various small operators.

In South Petherton, Cornhill House and the old H&C garage in Crown Lane were bought by Reg Beale who converted the garage into a Do-It-Yourself and central heating business. It was demolished in 1993 when he sold the land and the house. The St James Street premises eventually became a public car park, and at Barrington, the Royal Oak pub remains but the old bus garage is now a lawn mower and garden machinery showroom. At the end, H&C had fourteen vehicles and these were sold far and near. One, AEC Reliance TYD 122G was in public service until a couple of years ago, having been used on Sunday bus service 32 between Guildford and Dorking in Surrey, by Memory Lane Services. Several others survive in private ownership.

Safeway
Services

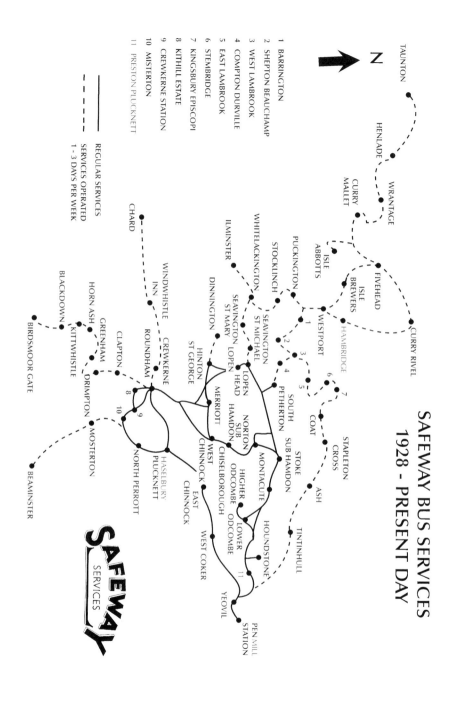

SAFEWAY BUS SERVICES
1928 - PRESENT DAY

1 BARRINGTON
2 SHEPTON BEAUCHAMP
3 WEST LAMBROOK
4 COMPTON DURVILLE
5 EAST LAMBROOK
6 STEMBRIDGE
7 KINGSBURY EPISCOPI
8 KITHILL ESTATE
9 CREWKERNE STATION
10 MISTERTON
11 PRESTON PLUCKNETT

—————— REGULAR SERVICES
- - - - - SERVICES OPERATED
           1 - 3 DAYS PER WEEK

N

SAFEWAY SERVICES

ten
From beer to buses

Compared to Hutchings & Cornelius, Safeway Services may have appeared at first sight as relatively staid and uninteresting. For much of their existence, they have only had one bus service and it was not until 1964 that the fleet size reached double figures. Yet they started with one bus, just like Alf Cornelius and Tommy Hutchings, and went on to provide the same ultra-reliable, friendly service which was rewarded with intense local loyalties in the villages they served *en route* to Yeovil. Unlike H&C, Safeway are still very much a part of South Petherton and remarkably still in the ownership of the same family after seventy-five years and many tribulations – not a bad record and one that the owner and staff should be very proud of.

In the early 1920s the landlord of the Bell Inn in St James Street in South Petherton was Gilbert Gunn. He had previously run pubs at Watchet and Blagdon Hill near Taunton. One day there was a fire and despite the attendance of the volunteer fire brigade based just across the road, it seems that damage was extensive. To avoid losing the pub's licence, Gunn served beer from outbuildings at the rear, until the refurbishment was completed in 1925. The pub was renamed The Brewers in 1984.

One of Gilbert Gunn's first pair of Dennis buses dating from 1928. Both had Waveney bodies – this one is thought to be XV 5430. It looks very well presented, as one might expect from the meticulous Gunn family. (Safeway collection)

Gilbert Gunn had a son Herbert and a daughter Veronica – known to many as Vera. Herbert served an apprenticeship at Westlands, during which time he was paid the princely sum of 2s 6d (12.5 pence) a week. He also had to pay 30s a week (£1.50) for his lodgings in Yeovil, and would come home to South Petherton at weekends on the Carriers Cart. His father funded the 30s a week cost of his tuition. Afterwards, Herbert went on to spend some time driving for National. He was a thorough and resourceful mechanic, which was to stand him in good stead, and around 1926 he convinced his sister of the business opportunity in starting a bus company and they decided to pool their savings in order to buy a second-hand bus which was located in Salisbury. They never got there due to a rail strike. Herbert stayed with National and Veronica moved away.

By 1928, Gilbert Gunn had moved to the Red House, on the corner of St James Street, Prigg Lane and Roundwell Street, and just across from where H&C were much later to have their main yard. An interesting building, it has a fountain marking Queen Victoria's Diamond Jubilee built into its wall on the Prigg Lane side and today it is Snell & Hutchinson's veterinary surgery. Gunn senior would say 'never buy a second-hand item if you want to provide a first-class service'. He therefore provided the financial assistance to enable his son to realise his ambition and a brand new twenty-seat Dennis G type with bodywork by Waveney was purchased from Ron Smith's showroom in London's Regent Street for £800. Pneumatic tyres were fitted, giving a distinct advantage over the solid-tyred vehicles then being used locally by National.

G. Gunn and Son started the Safeway service to Yeovil on 28 March 1928. South Petherton was only served by the first bus out and the last back, while for the rest of the day, Mondays to Saturdays, the Safeway service linked Hinton St George with Yeovil via Merriott, Crewkerne, Haselbury Plucknett, East Chinnock and West Coker, running through Yeovil town centre and terminating at Pen Mill Station. There were four trips each way, with an additional one on Saturday evenings when the bus awaited the end of the first house at the Palace cinema.

Father, mother and son were all involved with the business, with Herbert doing the driving. He was immediately in competition between Hinton St George and Yeovil with National service 22 and it was not long before the large concern began to make things difficult. Just over a month after starting his service, Herbert set off for Yeovil from Crewkerne one evening, followed by a National bus driven by Edward Coleman. The latter decided to pass Safeway on a bend on Barrow Hill near East Chinnock but unfortunately a lorry was coming the other way. The National bus then hit the lorry and bounced off into the back of the Safeway Dennis, breaking a window and denting a body panel. Coleman was fined £10 plus costs at the court hearing, where it came out that the National bus should have operated via Misterton and North Perrott, rather than the direct route out of Crewkerne used by Safeway. Seemingly, Coleman had been instructed by his superiors to shadow Safeway and to do his best to get past and reach the intending passengers first, something that the Chairman of the Bench thought should be investigated.

The next day, the Safeway service was back on the road with a bus hired from another local operator. Undaunted by this intimidation, Herbert Gunn was probably even more determined not to be run off the road by National and about six months after starting he purchased another Dennis G, again with a Waveney body. Unlike the first bus which was registered locally as YC 2376, the second was registered by the dealer in London as XV 5430. This enabled an increased service to be run, with alternate journeys starting from South Petherton via Lopen or from Hinton St George. Some journeys were diverted to also serve Crewkerne Station, Misterton and North Perrott.

Gilbert Gunn's home, 'The Red House' in South Petherton, was Safeway's first headquarters. Now a veterinary surgery, the car park on the site of H&C's St James Street premises can be seen on the far side of Prigg Lane. (Author)

A livery of red, maroon and cream was chosen and although the first bus was initially kept on a piece of land at Pitway, a move was made to the yard of the New Inn in Silver Street. There were some problems with the first bus, so Dennis Bros sent a man down to Somerset to work with Herbert Gunn on a solution, which included removing the original side-valve engine and replacing it with an overhead-valve type, making it the same as the later Dennis GL model. At that time, petrol was 6d (2.5 pence) a gallon. Making sure that the buses were ready for service next day was a challenge. Herbert Gunn's wife Gladys would assist through the night if necessary by holding a lantern so that Herbert and Jack Bryce, the first mechanic, could effect repairs.

eleven

Getting on with the job

In March 1931, another new Dennis was purchased. This was registered YD 1728, being one of their Dart model with a twenty-seat Strachan body. With a third bus in the fleet, a spare vehicle for the Yeovil service was available. Safeway made its application to the Traffic Commissioner under the Road Traffic Act 1930, for a licence for its existing bus service, without modification, in spring 1931. As it covered the same route between Crewkerne and Yeovil as Southern National, the latter objected, although between South Petherton and Crewkerne the two firms were not in conflict. The Commissioner's decision at the hearing in Taunton on 7 October that year, saw a licence being granted, although the section via Misterton and North Perrott was refused. However, it seems this decision was reversed, as the service continued to run unchanged, possibly after an appeal, although the details are now unclear.

Thus, Safeway settled down alongside Southern National as uneasy bedfellows, and while there were no joint arrangements, there were no protective picking-up and

The popularity of the Safeway bus service required a larger vehicle so this thirty-two-seat all-Dennis Lancet was delivered in May 1934. The posing drivers look smart in their caps with the 'Safeway' insignia. (R. Grimley collection)

In March 1931, the Safeway fleet became three in number with the arrival of YD 1728, this twenty-seat Dennis Dart with Strachan bodywork. It carries the livery of vehicles delivered in the early 1930s, being devoid of the usual cream. (Safeway collection)

Seen in recent times, this is Farnham House in North Street, South Petherton, next door to the Safeway depot. It was home to Veronica Gunn and her mother and subsequently to her brother Herbert and his family. (Author)

At the Pen Mill Station terminus of the Yeovil bus service is FYD 132, the first of two similar Duple-bodied utility Bedford OWBs which Herbert Gunn managed to obtain in 1943, when the allocation of new vehicles was strictly controlled. Seen in August 1952, these vehicles were withdrawn from service six years later. (A. Cross)

setting-down restrictions either. A reasonably co-ordinated timetable was developed over the years between the two operators with sensible spacing between their respective journeys.

The Safeway bus service was very popular and demand sometimes outstripped the small twenty-seat vehicles. Therefore the next new vehicle was a thirty-two-seater, being a Dennis Lancet which was registered on 1 June 1934, the day after the Cornelius and Hutchings businesses were formally combined. The registration number was YD 45, which is odd because this mark should have been issued in 1930, and seems to have been held back for some reason. Also acquired was a second-hand Dennis GL which previously belonged to a firm on Dennis' doorstep – A.T. Locke trading as Blue Saloon from Guildford. It had arrived by April 1936, probably earlier as it may have replaced the first Dennis G when the latter was sold in May 1935. The Gunns ordered another new Dennis Lancet, but in order to obtain earlier delivery, they accepted one with dual purpose, rear-entrance thirty-two-seat bodywork which came in October 1936. CYA 105 had in fact been removed from a batch then in build for the East Kent Road Car Co.

To ease the strain on the family, Gilbert Gunn asked his daughter Veronica to return home in 1934 and assist with the business, becoming conductress, cleaner and general helper. During the 1930s the vehicles were transferred to some ground in North Street which was rented from Tom Walter – a farmyard with some buildings fronting the road, adjacent to Anstice's Bakery. When Herbert Gunn married, he and his wife lived in a cottage in St James Street. In 1938 Gilbert Gunn died and the business became a partnership between his son, daughter and Jessica, his widow, with the licence for the bus service being changed to the new entity of H.R., J. and V. Gunn from December of that year.

The last new vehicle before the outbreak of war came in June 1939, being a twenty-seat Dennis Pike coach. This was owned for eighteen years, while the two original Lancets lasted sixteen and seventeen years respectively. Longevity of ownership within the fleet became the norm, due largely to the skill and resourcefulness of Herbert Gunn and his mechanics, including Joe Frost. The latter joined Safeway in October 1947 on leaving the Forces, and was a key member of the staff for some forty years. They were both regular drivers too and this often provided a useful insight into problems requiring workshop rectification. Like H&C, Safeway found it impossible to obtain new vehicles in the first years of the war and Herbert Gunn was probably none too happy about having to make do with a Tilling Stevens thirty-two-seat coach with Harrington body, originally delivered to Alexandra Coaches of Portsmouth back in 1932. This brute of a vehicle needed three men to start it – one on the huge starting handle and one on each end of a rope that had to be attached to it. It would only do four miles per gallon and latterly was only used on Saturdays. Two Bedford OWB utility thirty-two-seaters were obtained in 1943. Safeway were undertaking some contract work and the bus service was very busy. Vehicle and driver availability may not have been good as during summer and early autumn 1943, Wakes of Sparkford were covering various journeys on the bus service on Safeway's behalf.

twelve
Success and frustration

The period between 1946 and 1953 saw several developments in the business. The first post-war vehicle was GYC 330, an attractive Bedford OB bus with Duple bodywork delivered in March 1946, while FOT 432 was a second-hand example of the same type but with a coach body by Wadhams which was purchased in August 1948. Then in June 1949 came the last Dennis (until 2001!) – a Lancet J3 with a thirty-three-seat coach body by Readings. It was also the last half-cab vehicle to be acquired. Herbert Gunn was keen on keeping one driver on each vehicle, and Bill Leverick was the only person for some time allowed to drive the new Lancet. It was active until 1969 but was not sold. In 1985 it was refurbished by Joe Frost and Alfred White, re-registered ASV 900 and was then taken to various bus rallies for several years, but was not licensed as a Public Service vehicle. It remains at South Petherton in Safeway ownership.

FYD 922, a second-hand wartime Bedford OWB was purchased in 1949 from Furslands at Bridgwater, followed in October 1950 by the delivery of a new Bedford OB twenty-nine-seat coach with standard Duple Vista bodywork, registered MYB 33. Safeway regularly used coaches on the bus service and this OB lasted in the fleet for twenty-four years – Herbert and Veronica made their vehicles last with careful maintenance. When MYB 33 arrived, the 1934 Lancet and the Tilling Stevens were withdrawn.

About 1947, Safeway Services applied to the Traffic Commissioner for a new stage carriage service from Crewkerne to Taunton via Ilminster and Ilton. The latter place then had no bus service but there was a station on the railway line between Taunton and Chard, while Safeway would not have carried passengers locally between Ilminster and Taunton, to offer protection to Southern National. There would only have been three journeys a day, but Southern National objected. There was much local support for Safeway, including the press and three Members of Parliament. Yet at the hearing, the licence was granted to Southern National and despite engaging the services of a QC, Safeway's appeal was unsuccessful and they were left with a bill for £800, a fair sum of money in those days.

After the war, Safeway regularly provided vehicles to the army on a private-hire basis for the movement of military personnel at Houndstone Camp to sporting and social events. They also ran contract journeys from the camp into Yeovil until 1951 when army funds were no longer available. With the introduction of national service, there was a large demand for transport for weekend leave. Safeway were commissioned to run regular journeys to Birmingham on a private-hire basis costing each soldier £1 return, and there were also occasional trips to London. The fare was very favourable compared to using the train, which was slow and inconvenient for long cross-country journeys from Yeovil and took away too much precious time out of the weekend leave allowed.

In February 1952, the Gunns applied unsuccessfully for express-service licences from Houndstone to Birmingham and London, and despite an appeal, the licences were awarded to Darch & Willcox Ltd of Martock. The proprietors of that business had both

In Yeovil in April 1960 is FOT 432, a Bedford OB with Wadham coach body, which was purchased in August 1948 from the large Hampshire independent operator – Creamline of Bordon. (R. Lee)

been servicemen and although they had four modern coaches and the level of service they gave was highly regarded by the camp authorities, the Gunns felt that due to their other good work there, they should have had 'established' operator status and been granted the licences. The whole question of Forces-leave services and the way Traffic Commissioners selected one applicant over another became a national issue in the coach industry and was widely reported in the trade press.

In 1948, Safeway started an express service to the Westlands Aircraft Factory, along similar lines to that run by H&C. It started at Crewkerne and ran via Haselbury Plucknett, East Chinnock and West Coker and originally also served the village of Hardington, but the additional mileage involved and declining patronage meant that this detour was abandoned subsequently. Only weekly tickets were issued and the service survived until the 1960s. A successful application was made to extend two journeys on the bus service beyond Hinton St George to Dinnington on Wednesdays and Saturdays and this started on 8 August 1949, while certain journeys were diverted in Crewkerne to also serve Severalls Estate at school times.

Farnham House in North Street was purchased by the business from the Anstice family, and Veronica and her mother moved in. Also included were the adjacent stone buildings which had been used by Walrond Anstice as a bakery, including flour storage, dough-mixing area and ovens. These were converted into offices and staff restrooms, while the parking area was purchased from Mrs Walter, including some more land.

Planning permission was eventually obtained for a new garage building to replace the original somewhat primitive structure. It was built by Blight & White of Plymouth in the early 1950s, being high enough to accommodate double-deckers. These were never owned, but those of H&C would be brought in for MOT inspection. In later years a lower extension was added at the front so that each bay could accommodate two eleven-metre vehicles, with an overall capacity of twelve buses or coaches.

The business became a partnership of H.R. & V. Gunn by January 1952. When Jessica Gunn died, Herbert and his family moved into Farnham House, while Veronica took residence in the converted upstairs living accommodation above the adjacent offices in the old bakehouse. This flat was appropriately named 'the Lookout' as she could keep a sharp eye on what was going on in the yard. By this time, she was handling most of the administrative work for the business and showing shrewd commercial acumen. During the day she was out as a conductress, often with her brother driving.

The second bus on the service was conducted by Cissie Gayleard who was a real South Petherton character and joined Safeway shortly after the war. Cissie (real name Maude) and Gwen were twin nieces of Bill Gayleard the saddler and charabanc proprietor. They are well remembered locally for their individualistic unmarried way of life and their land became a haven for unwanted ponies, as they had found horses their main interest from an early age. Gwen was a postwoman and she used to deliver the mail by pony and trap, at her own somewhat slow pace, around Compton Durville and the Lambrooks. The sisters

By 1946, new vehicle specification was more relaxed, as demonstrated by this thirty-two-seat Bedford OB with Duple bodywork. This attractive Safeway bus is laying over at the parking ground used in Yeovil by Safeway and Wakes, and shared with the Yeovil Caravans business. (Author's collection)

The wartime utility Bedford OWBs sometimes gained replacement upholstered seats, to replace the original wooden slatted variety. One such was FYD 922 which Safeway purchased from Furslands of Bridgwater in November 1949. (R. Lee)

would drive their trap to Crewkerne to collect animal feed and had no hesitation in hitching their pony to a 'No Waiting' sign, or driving it the wrong way around The Square in South Petherton when it was made one-way, just as a matter of principle.

On the school run, the children would leave the bus by the rear emergency exit and then come round to the front again until Cissie thought it would burst. In the busy years after the war, she would stand at the side of the bus, and by asking people 'to move right down', could pack up to 100 people into it on a good day. On occasion, some wag would ring the bell and leave her standing by the gasworks, so the driver had to wait for her to catch up. One evening, outside the Gaumont cinema in Yeovil, Cissie was presiding over a healthy standing load of boarding passengers. She was approached by a policeman who said, 'Come on Ciss, you know you can't load all that lot on'. To this she replied in her inimitable way, 'Surely you be doing something better than running after me!' Having defeated the constabulary, the bus departed.

The schoolchildren who travelled with Safeway knew well enough that any misbehaviour or cheekiness would result in a clip round the ear with the ticket rack, or being put off the vehicle to find their own way to their destination!

In the early 1960s, two Londoners on holiday in the district spent much time riding on Cissie's bus and were so taken by her consideration for the passengers in such a different way as to what one would find in London, that they telephoned Miss Gunn to tell her how much they had enjoyed themselves.

On one occasion, Gwen Gayleard's horse shied, breaking the wooden shafts of the trap. Joe Frost arrived at work to be instructed by Herbert Gunn to take it into the garage and effect some repairs, most likely as a community service, so the mail could still be delivered!

In October 1950, Safeway took delivery of MYB 33, an example of the ubiquitous Bedford OB with a twenty-nine-seat Duple Vista coach body. In the fleet for a remarkable twenty-four years, it is parked here outside the Dolphin Hotel in Ilminster in October 1963. (R. Lee)

Possibly following approaches to various local operators from the villages south of Crewkerne, two separate applications were made in October 1952. H.A. Vincent of Thorncombe asked for a Friday afternoon round trip into Crewkerne via Birdsmoorgate, Blackdown, Kittwhistle, Horn Ash, Greenham, Drimpton and Clapton, while Safeway Services sought a facility only from Drimpton and Clapton on Tuesday and Friday afternoons and Saturday evenings. A similar route on similar days had been run by Harrison's Motor Coaches of Clapton until 1950, when Will Harrison sold out to Wessex Coaches.

The Traffic Commissioner granted Vincents' service a short-period licence from 27 October, pending a hearing at Bridgwater in January 1953 when both companies counter-objected. In the event, the Gunns were successful and the licence eventually granted allowed the Tuesday service to start at Greenham and the Friday and Saturday journeys to cover the full route from Birdsmoorgate, but not Thorncombe. Safeway started on 28 March 1953 and usually used one of the small Bedfords which were quite adequate for the loadings, with the driver collecting the fares.

When Miss Gunn occupied the flat above the Safeway office, she named it 'the Lookout'. The letterbox on the main gate, with her name on it was still in situ as such three years after her death. (Author)

thirteen
New opportunities

It was to be nearly five years before the next vehicle was purchased, as it was in June 1955 when a forty-three-seat Duple-bodied coach on an AEC Reliance chassis arrived – TYD 755 was the largest owned to date. Used mainly on coaching duties, it was also used on the Yeovil bus service on Saturday afternoons. The 1939 Dennis Pike was sold in August 1957 to become a mobile shop in the area. It was still in an excellent condition mechanically and included in the sale were various spare parts remaining in stock. A year later the original wartime Bedford OWBs were retired, being parked in the back of the garage until the mid-1960s, yielding spares for other Bedfords.

Driver Bill Leverick and conductress Cissie Gayleard, in characteristic working attire. Cissie brandishes a rack of Bell Punch tickets and wears the punch machine on a strap. (Commercial Motor)

Like H&C, Safeway turned to AEC for its larger new vehicles when Dennis ended production of the standard Lancet model. TYD 755 was delivered in June 1955 and had a forty-three-seat Duple body, the highest capacity owned so far. It was in stock for twenty-three years. In the background are the offices with Veronica Gunn's flat above. (Commercial Motor)

The first diesel-engined Bedford at Safeway was MVA 832, with Duple Midland bus bodywork, acquired after use by Heybrook Bay Motor Services in 1959. The location is the starting point of the Yeovil bus service in South Petherton, on the corner of St James Street and Palmer Street. In the background, North Street leads towards the Safeway depot. (R. Lee)

The new bus service into Crewkerne was a disappointment, being somewhat unremunerative. In the autumn of 1955 it was cut back to start at Horn Ash and withdrawn entirely on Tuesdays. Subsequently, the Saturday evening journeys were given up and finally the Friday journeys were discontinued on 2 December 1961. In June 1955, the Yeovil bus service had its South Petherton terminal point re-designated as North Street Corner –opposite the Coke Memorial Chapel and near the garage. This replaced the time-honoured departure point in The Square.

In January 1959, bus dealers Barnard & Barnard were collecting two vehicles from Heybrook Bay Motor Services near Plymouth and thought that Herbert Gunn might be interested. They stopped off at South Petherton so that both vehicles could be tried, with the result that one, registered MVA 832, was purchased. This was a forty-seat Bedford SBO bus with Duple Midland bodywork, originally owned by Hutchisons of Overtown in Scotland.

The next Bedford purchased was a petrol-engined SBG with unusual thirty-six-seat rear-entrance bodywork by Owen. PXC 539 came from Super Coaches of Upminster and cannot have been successful as it only lasted about a year and a half. To cater for small groups of private-hire customers, a fourteen-seat Reading-bodied Karrier was purchased in 1960, registered 600 GYC. In January 1961 the first of several vehicles to be purchased from the similarly named Safeguard Coaches of Guildford arrived – UPK 615, another Bedford/Duple Midland bus. Safeguard's livery was conveniently red and cream, only lacking Safeway's maroon roof and this meant that they could be used without a repaint being necessary. The next bus was also from Safeguard – an AEC Reliance with a handsome forty-four-seat Burlingham body registered 200 APB. It became one of Safeway's most well-known vehicles and lasted for nearly twenty years, being sold for active preservation on withdrawal in 1982. A man in the 1960s had moved from Guildford

In the Borough, Yeovil is Safeway's PXC 539, a petrol-engined Bedford SBG with uncommon Owen bodywork with rear entrance. Arriving from Super Coaches of Upminster in 1959, it was only retained for eighteen months. (R. Lee)

Although not a particularly treasured member of the fleet, this fourteen-seat Karrier with Reading coach body was owned for fourteen years from 1960, when it was bought new to cater for small private-hire parties. Nowadays, a fourteen-seat vehicle would be a far less substantial standard minibus, such as a Ford Transit or LDV Convoy. (Safeway collection)

In Yeovil in February 1962 are (left to right): Bedford OB MYB 33, Bedford SBO UPK 615 and Dennis Lancet J3 ETP 184. The SBO, with Duple Midland body was, in January 1961, the first of several vehicles to come from Safeguard of Guildford. The Lancet, with Reading thirty-three-seat coachwork was bought new in June 1949 and is still owned today. (R. Lee)

Synonymous with the bus service in the 1960s and 1970s was 200 APB, acquired from Safeguard in November 1962. This attractive AEC Reliance with Burlingham body is seen shortly after arrival in Somerset and carries its original red and cream livery, with the Safeguard fleet name insignia painted out. The driver was Bob Tomlin. Today, it is once again back in Guildford with its first owner, for special-occasion use. (Commercial Motor)

Taking the active Safeway fleet into double figures for the first time were two Duple-bodied Bedford SB coaches acquired with the Venture Coaches business of Ernie Giles. Still in Giles' cream and orange livery, LBK 766 (an SBG model) was resting in Yeovil in February 1964, a month after purchase. (R. Lee)

SOR 117, the other Giles coach, a Bedford SB3 with distinctive 'butterfly' radiator grille, picks up in Yeovil for Crewkerne and South Petherton. (R. Lee)

Another Bedford SB3 which was quite similar to SOR 117 acquired from Giles, was 7718 HK. It came in July 1964 to replace Bedford OB FOT 432. It carries the revised Safeway coach livery, with more cream than that formerly used. (R. Lee)

to Yeovil and found himself going to work on the same bus! The wheel turned full circle in December 2001 when Safeguard acquired it for sentimental reasons and returned it to its original home town.

The winter weather of 1962/3 was particularly cold with much snow over a prolonged period and it was noted by a resident of Merriott that Southern National service 7 became very erratic and unreliable, but Safeway never once let the village down; to do so would have been unthinkable for the Gunns.

By this time it was becoming more apparent that car ownership was reducing the use made of the bus service, although it was still profitable. Miss Gunn was particularly concerned by car owners who pulled up at bus stops and offered lifts to people waiting there, thus decreasing her revenue. If that continued she warned that small companies would be forced to ask for subsidies costing the tax payer millions of pounds – a concept she was staunchly against. Safeway saw the need for diversification and perhaps as far as car owners were concerned, it was a matter of 'if you can't beat them, join them'. To this end, Safeway Services purchased the Lopen Head Filling Station on the A303, just on the Ilminster side of the South Petherton turn off near Watergore, and when not involved with buses, Herbert Gunn would go there to assist with petrol sales.

Herbert was a 'stage-carriage' man – you knew where you were with daily revenue coming in all year, so it probably took a fair amount of persuasion on Veronica's part when she convinced him that good business could be had by running advertised Excursions and Tours. To that end they purchased the coaching operations of Ernest Giles of South

Apart from a second-hand Bedford SB8 coach in 1969, no other vehicles were acquired from 1964 until 1973! Then, Safeway significantly modernised its front-line bus stock with two new Leyland Leopard heavyweight chassis with Willowbrook bodies, which looked very smart in the traditional red, maroon and cream livery. PYC 746L had coach-style seats when new, and is *en route* to Yeovil. (R. Stenning)

Petherton, who traded as Venture Coaches, which included an excursion licence for various destinations, picking up at South Petherton, Hinton St George, Merriott, Lopen and East Lambrook. His two coaches, which were petrol-engined, Duple-bodied Bedford SBs being so typical of the small coach proprietor (registered LBK 766 and SOR 117) joined the Safeway fleet and initially ran in their old livery of cream with orange lining. The orange was later repainted red, thus introducing a new Safeway coach livery. Also transferred was a school contract from Chiselborough and Norton to the school at Stoke sub Hamdon, which joined that already operated from Tintinhull, Ash and Bower Hinton to Stoke, one to schools in Ilminster and one around South Petherton village to the local infant school in St James Street. Also by that time, Safeway were running a private works contract from Ilminster, Hinton St George and Merriott to the Van Heusen shirt factory in Crewkerne.

Ernie Giles was born in South Petherton in 1902. After leaving school, he started work as an apprentice in 1916 at Sibley Engineering's Parrett Works between Petherton and Martock. After the First World War he went to work at Parson's garage, and in the early 1920s he started running a fourteen-seat charabanc which he made himself. Apparently, a Model T Ford body was cut in half, an extra part spliced in, and then mounted on the Ford chassis, with pneumatic tyres. Originally kept at the Crown Inn stables, it later moved to Parson's garage.

In 1929 Ernie borrowed £25 from his sister to buy some land. In 1931 he opened his new Harp Road garage in South Petherton where he repaired cars and sold petrol, and in 1937 he bought the thirteen-seat Reo Bluebird YA 9376 from Messrs Walter and Parsons, together with their licence for Excursions and Tours from South Petherton. During the 1930s, Bronc Carter would take the local schoolgirls to Castle School for cookery and laundry instruction in the Reo.

The Reo was replaced in December 1937 with a twenty-five-seat Bedford WTB, followed by two Bedford OB coaches – JYB 856 in 1948 and LYC 188 in 1950, which were supplanted by the two SBs. When the coaches were sold to Safeway, Giles kept the garage business until 1969 when he retired. His sons took over but the site was soon to be threatened with compulsory purchase as it was on the planned alignment of the A303 Ilminster bypass. The Department of Transport bought the garage but then changed their mind on the route of the road, so the filling station continued under new ownership.

It was not long before Miss Gunn had expanded the range of tours offered, with more attractive and marketable destinations, and extra picking-up points were granted at North Perrott and Haselbury Plucknett. Another Bedford SB/Duple coach with petrol engine was acquired in July 1964 to replace the Wadham-bodied OB. Herbert Gunn was very happy with petrol engines rather than diesel but wished that manufacturers would improve their efficiency. He would have had them in all the vehicles if fuel consumption could have been reduced by 25-30 per cent, as they were quieter, easier to service, reduced bodywork wear and had an acceptable time period between major overhauls. Yet all further Safeway vehicles had realistically to be diesels, starting with a Bedford SB8 with Leyland engine and Harrington coach body which came from Sewards of Dalwood in Devon in June 1969 to replace the oldest of the Giles' coaches.

fourteen
David and Goliath

In spring 1967, local loyalty and support increased to an unprecedented level and Safeway achieved fame nationally when there was a disagreement with Southern National over fare increases. At that time, when an operator successfully applied to raise fares, which was unfortunately commonplace, other operators running along parallel sections of route were expected to 'come into line'. This time when National gained permission, Miss Gunn did not wish to follow suit. She had done so reluctantly in the past but thought it was time to make a stand. She strongly believed that raising fares was not a good way of making rural bus services secure and thought that her customers had reached a limit to what they were prepared to pay and that customer resistance would ultimately put small companies not receiving subsidy out of business. The way forward was to operate shrewdly and economise on unnecessary practices as much as possible.

Unfortunately, the licence for the Yeovil bus service was coming up for renewal and because Miss Gunn would not bring her fares into line, National lodged a formal objection. This may have also been in retaliation for a complaint made by Safeway in January 1967 that the re-timing of a journey by Southern National on service 7 resulted

Leyland Leopard RYA 676L lasted twenty years. Its destination blind leaves little doubt as to where it is going, as it waits for time on the corner of North Street in South Petherton. Standing in front of the imposing Coke Methodist church is one of Southern National's Bristol LH/Plaxton coaches which were often used on bus services. The photograph dates from August 1983. (G. Wise)

Acquired from Wakes of Sparkford in 1974 was TYD 888, an AEC Reliance/Duple coach, nineteen years after the arrival of similar TYD 755 purchased new at about the same time as Wakes took delivery of TYD 888. (Author's collection)

Standing in the depot yard is UAR 940M, a Leyland Leopard with Plaxton Panorama Elite coachwork. In later life it was fitted with bus seats. Miss Gunn used to complain that coach seat upholstery sometimes got stained by blood from meat purchased by her passengers in town. Evident is lettering applied for Safeway's golden jubilee. (Coach & Bus Week)

Yet another former Safeguard vehicle was HPG 30N, a Leyland Leopard/Duple Dominant coach, obtained in October 1978. Like many Safeway coaches it was used on the bus service as evidenced by the ticket machine mounted alongside the driver. Setright tickets had replaced the original Bell Punch type. (Coach & Bus Week)

in both companies' buses leaving Crewkerne for Merriott together at a certain time in the afternoon. Safeway sought the support of local councils for the licence renewal, the matter appeared in the national press and Miss Gunn was interviewed by television news. The Traffic Commissioner was spared a decision as Southern National withdrew their objection at the hearing in August, another example of how the small South Petherton independents held their own against the mighty state-owned National.

When the Yeovil Bus Station opened in May 1968, the Safeway service called there and it was used for parking between journeys. Previously, they had used a parking area shared with a caravan business just off the road leading to Pen Mill, and jointly owned by the Gunns and Wakes Services of Sparkford. From autumn 1970, the Yeovil service was withdrawn from Dinnington due to negligible usage.

The advent of Bus Grant, available from the Government for the purchase of new vehicles for bus services, initiated a transformation of Safeway's fleet profile. Whereas most small operators bought the latest type of what they knew best – usually Bedfords – Safeway went for heavyweight Leyland Leopards which Herbert Gunn thought would stand up better to the rigours of stage-carriage operation and also on longer distance coach work. In spring 1973 the first new purpose-built buses since 1946 arrived. Two Leopards had Willowbrook bodywork to the well known BET design. PYC 746L had fifty-one coach seats while RYC 676L had fifty-one ordinary bus seats, and they became the mainstay of the Yeovil service. When a new coach was needed in May 1974 a Plaxton bodied Volvo B58 was tried – a chassis type then newly available to UK operators but was only kept for about ten years, being sold in pursuit of a Leyland standardisation policy. In contrast, the same month saw the arrival of TYD 888, an AEC Reliance with Duple body acquired from Wakes, being very similar to the example purchased new by Safeway in 1955.

Sadly, Herbert Gunn died in December 1977 after a short illness, with his wife inheriting his share of the business. The filling station at Lopen Head had already been sold to the Goddard family before Herbert's death. Veronica Gunn then purchased Gladys Gunn's share in the business and thus became sole proprietor of Safeway Services.

In 1976 the Yeovil bus service was diverted via Kit Hill Estate in Crewkerne while in September 1977 a schoolday service was introduced between Lopen Head and Ilminster via the Seavingtons and Whitelackington, this being licensed so that the general public could be carried too, although that situation only lasted until December 1978. Safeway celebrated their fiftieth anniversary on 28 March 1978, with no fares being charged that day but with any voluntary payments being donated to local hospitals. This was even reported in the *Daily Telegraph*! Also, there was a special issue of Bell Punch-style tickets.

A short-period licence was obtained for an experimental service on Fridays from Chard which connected with the Yeovil service at Crewkerne, with through fares available. Running direct via the A30, it lasted from 14 July until 29 December 1978. In spring 1978, Western National reduced their service 467 Yeovil–Crewkerne–Hinton St George (renumbered from 7 in 1969) from six journeys to three, so Safeway added some peak hour and school-time journeys to their South Petherton–Yeovil route in compensation. This was followed by the total withdrawal by Western National in December that year, allowing further consolidation of the Safeway service.

Two coaches, second-hand Leyland Leopards, came in 1978, including HPG 30N – the third vehicle to come from Safeguard of Guildford. Thus the stage was set for a major milestone in Safeway's seventy-four-year history.

fifteen
New pastures and old worries

Veronica Gunn's decision to pick up some of the pieces of the Hutchings & Cornelius business was probably coloured by a mixture of commercial opportunity and concern for the local community, both being positive attributes of Safeway. She probably also did not relish the prospect of Western National returning to the South Petherton/Crewkerne –Yeovil routes, with further potential for competitive tactics. As well as acquiring the bus services and vehicles mentioned earlier, Safeway offered employment to five H&C drivers, including Jack Bindon, who just drove the Friday Ilminster/Yeovil service having retired from full-time work with H&C. Until then, all the office work was undertaken by Miss Gunn herself, which when she was out on the road doing conductress duties meant mainly in the evening or at weekends. Mrs Gladys Gunn was also a conductress and had increased her duties so that Miss Gunn could spend more time on administrative matters.

Business expansion meant that additional assistance was needed and so Christine Hodgkinson, H&C's receptionist, also moved to Safeway and is still with them twenty-four years later. Initially, the only change made to the bus services was the withdrawal of the late evening journeys on the former H&C Yeovil route due to the low level of patronage.

Making the move 'up the road' in South Petherton in April 1979 was FPC 15J, an AEC Reliance/Willowbrook bus taken in by Safeway from H&C a month before the latter ceased trading. This bus too started life on bus services in Guildford with Safeguard. (G. Gillberry)

Brutonian's Wednesday and Saturday service from South Petherton to Taunton did not last long as in October 1979 it was taken over by Safeway. From 12 December, an additional bus was provided on Wednesdays from Crewkerne, Merriott and Lopen, connecting at Lopen Head with the South Petherton–Taunton bus. For the return trip, the one bus covered both South Petherton and Crewkerne as required, the whole operation fitting neatly around school transport activities. The service was reduced from 29 April 1981 to run from Crewkerne to Taunton only, just on Wednesdays, and apart from the diversion made by 1986 to take the route through Hambridge and Curry Rivel instead of Isle Brewers, (to allow the use of an eleven-metre-long vehicle) it survived virtually unaltered until 21 March 2001 when it was withdrawn due to declining patronage. Somerset County Council then stepped in and awarded a contract to Berrys Coaches of Taunton to continue it.

From 16 January 1980, Safeway started an experimental Wednesday morning shoppers' bus into South Petherton from Shepton Beauchamp, West Lambrook, Kingsbury Episcopi and East Lambrook, but this stopped running during the following year. It was also in 1980 that a Transport Act was enacted by the Government which allowed for the 'deregulation' of the coach industry, and also paved the way for the full deregulation of bus services six years later. Thus, Safeway's Excursions and Tours no longer required a licence, allowing much more flexibility in what trips could be offered in response to local demands.

Somewhat unusually, the next vehicle purchase was PXS 820N, a Ford R1114 with Willowbrook bus body, acquired in April 1980 from Graham of Paisley, but only lasting just over six years in the fleet, in comparison to the fifteen to twenty years often accomplished with the heavier Leylands. The Ford was regarded as an aberration – the least said the better. It even broke down when Joe Frost collected it, and had to be towed to South Petherton!

Protruding from one of the converted original farm buildings fronting North Street, at the Safeway depot, is VYC 852W, a Leyland Leopard, new in 1981. Its folding bus-type door meant it could be used on a full range of work. (Author)

New in 1982 was YYA 122X, another Leyland Leopard, this time with Plaxton Supreme bodywork. (Author)

Destined to have a long life in the fleet, TYD 911W, a Leyland Leopard with Duple Dominant bus body was a front-line performer on the Yeovil services. When delivered in 1980, it was Safeway's first new vehicle for six years and lasted until 2001. (Author)

The first new vehicle since 1974 came in November 1980, a sixty-one-seat Leyland Leopard bus with a Duple Dominant body, registered TYD 911W. Towards the rear, it had three seats on one side of the aisle, and two on the other. This was followed in April 1981 by VYC 852W, another new Leopard but with a Duple Dominant coach body. The arrival of former London Transport AEC Merlin registered AML 614H was something of a surprise. With a fifty-seat Metro Cammell bus body, this was one of a large number delivered to London in the late 1960s and early 1970s, where they only had a short life and notorious reliability problems. Opinions on the merits of London Transport's MB614 while it was at Safeway were mixed but it was sold in 1989 having spent long periods in the garage. When in good form, it ran well and was powerful, but its mechanical and electrical complexities were a challenge!

The Thursday service from Houndstone Camp to Yeovil was withdrawn after 30 December 1982 , the Crewkerne to Yeovil via Montacute service was diverted to also serve Merriott from 15 June 1987 while from 1 October 1988 the Yeovil services no longer terminated at Pen Mill, but at the bus station for all journeys.

Between 1982 and 1996, all vehicle acquisitions were Leylands – eight Leopards and five Tigers. One of the Leopards and three of the Tigers were purchased new – all

Somewhat unusual for Safeway, and rather temperamental, was this former London Transport AEC Merlin rear-engined single-decker with Metro Cammell bodywork. It stayed nearly eight years and by the time of this photograph from 1990, it was owned by a dealer and was on loan to Hants & Sussex (B.S. Williams Ltd) of Emsworth, who had a number of them. (A. Lambert)

coaches, the last new delivery being Duple-bodied Tiger E565 YYA in April 1988. A colder financial climate has meant that since then all vehicles have had previous owners. Noteworthy among the Leopards was VPF 42M, with attractive Willowbrook bus body – the last purchase from Safeguard, NPA 228W which had once been used by London Country on Green Line services in the London area and HHU 42V and FDC 417V which although having Plaxton Supreme coach bodies were fitted with bus-type seating. Also of interest is GIB 5970, which started life as a coach but had been re-bodied with a Willowbrook Warrior bus body before it arrived at Safeway.

The Transport Act 1985 allowed for the 'deregulation' of the bus industry. Bus services would no longer require a licence, under normal circumstances there could be no objections lodged and hearings were no longer held. Instead, operators had to register their services with the Commissioner at least forty-two days in advance of their intention to start, amend or cancel a service. Bus companies could therefore control the destiny of their own networks and make their own commercial decisions in respect of services they ran without Local Authority financial support. In spring 1986, operators had to register those services they wished to run on a commercial basis from 26 October of that year, so that the County Councils could decide whether they wished to supplement them by securing 'socially necessary' services through a competitive tendering process. As Safeway's services were all 'commercial', they were registered and continued much as before. However, Dorset County Council contracted Safeway to run a service from Beaminster and Mosterton on Mondays and Thursdays which would offer connections for Yeovil at Crewkerne on the outward journey and at Misterton on the return trip. This was something of an experiment and it only lasted from 27 October 1986 until 30 April 1987.

An October morning in the village of Merriott in 1990. Safeway's VPF 42M, a Willowbrook-bodied Leyland Leopard is *en route* from Yeovil to Crewkerne. Another former Safeguard bus, it was quite similar to the two examples bought new in 1973. (J. Marsh)

Safeway's first Leyland Tiger, A983 NYC, with Plaxton body, bought new in 1983 and still owned. It is making the tight turn into the depot from North Street, after the morning school run. (Author)

Willowbrook was certainly a favoured make of body with the Gunns and this was their first with a coach body, the Crusader model. C744 JYA, a 1986 Leyland Tiger is at the Showbus Rally at Woburn in the same year. (Source unknown)

Miss Gunn was very worried about the potential effect of unregulated competition which could be suffered by small operators, particularly in rural areas. She was probably quite right with her view that car ownership had diminished bus usage to such an extent that another operator trying to compete on her services would go out of business and so would she, to the detriment of the local community and the coffers of the County Council which would have to pay dearly to sort out the mess and provide basic subsidised services in lieu of those she ran with no call on the public purse. Subsequent local events demonstrated that she was correct to be concerned. Various generations of the Gunn family had been staunch Conservatives, but Veronica had become disenchanted with their transport policies on bus-service deregulation. She transferred her support to Yeovil MP Paddy Ashdown, whose own children travelled, coincidentally, on one of Safeway's school contracts. An interesting aside is that apparently customers on some of Safeway's excursions to London enjoyed access to the Public Gallery of the House of Commons, this being facilitated by Paddy Ashdown.

sixteen
Celebration and attack

For many years, Veronica Gunn had been well known and respected in the bus industry for her forthright views on how to run a successful bus company and on various topical issues connected with passenger transport. She kept a sharp eye on wasteful and inefficient practices, especially in the larger companies and strongly advocated a climate where bus services could run without subsidy. She was proud that the only outside financial support she received was from Yeovil District Council for reimbursement for their Senior Citizens Concessionary Fare scheme, especially as it was estimated that about 75 per cent of Safeway customers were pensioners or children travelling at reduced fares. As has been seen, her contention was that higher fares were not the answer to making country bus services pay.

At one time she had the distinction of being the only female member of the national committee of the Passenger Vehicle Operators Association as well as having been vice-chair of their Western Area committee. She appeared on television in a debate which included Barbara Castle, the Transport Minister, where she advocated the case against nationalisation. Prior to that, Miss Gunn had little experience of television, having never owned one or had the time to watch one.

Veronica was one of seven people invited at short notice to the BBC studio in Plymouth to put the viewpoint of the small privately-run business. Mrs Castle was in London and appeared in Plymouth on a monitor screen, so they could observe someone help her remove her coat, thereby ruffling her hair. Mrs Castle retorted, quite crossly: 'Oh my hair!

Safeway bought their last new vehicle in 1988, this Leyland Tiger/Duple E565 YYA, being posed in the yard at South Petherton by driver Eric Rice. (Coach & Bus Week)

In the early 1990s, Willowbrook were placing new Warrior bus bodies onto older chassis, in lieu of original coach bodies. Leyland Leopard XCW 153R of 1977 received its new body in 1992 and was re-registered GIB 5970 before joining Safeway. (Author)

The final Leyland Tiger for Safeway was F202 HSO with Plaxton Paramount body, acquired in 1993 and previously with well-known Scottish operator Parks of Hamilton. It sets off along North Street to perform a school contract. (Author)

Second-hand Leyland Leopard/Plaxton coach HHU 42V had Supreme Express bodywork and was fitted with bus seats while with Safeway. (Author)

Do please be careful!' So Veronica said, 'Whoever minds about her hair? I'm sure I don't!' When Mrs Castle glowered through the monitor, it was only then that Veronica realised that she could also be seen and heard in London. As the only female bus operator of the seven, Veronica was the last to speak. She had noticed how Mrs Castle, like many politicians, had responded lengthily to questions, thus preventing anybody else putting their point of view. Determined to have her say, Veronica succinctly put her case for the small independent bus operator against nationalisation, and how the public would be left 'high and dry'. Mrs Castle only had time for the briefest of replies, which proved that nobody got the better of Miss Gunn. Off air, Mrs Castle said, 'My dear, you have nothing to worry about', to which Veronica replied while wagging her finger, 'I'll hold you to that!'.

Veronica attributed the survival of Safeway to hard work, personal service, attention to detail and familiarity with the needs of the local community. To her staff, she was a fair employer and commanded loyalty. She was a parish councillor in South Petherton for some years. Thus there was no shortage of nominations leading up to the announcement in June 1987 that she was to receive the MBE for 'services to transport' in the Queen's Birthday Honours List.

Southern National withdrew from a number of their services in south Somerset from 1 September 1987, and some in Safeway's area passed to Wakes Services. The latter started service 10 from Yeovil to Ilminster via Martock, South Petherton, Shepton Beauchamp and Barrington, and service 40 from Yeovil to Taunton on Saturdays via Montacute, Martock, South Petherton, Barrington and Curry Rivel. These were joined from 16 November by service 41 from Yeovil to Taunton on Mondays to Fridays via South Petherton, Shepton Beauchamp, Barrington and Ilton. In 1989 the contracts for these services passed back to Southern National, except that Wakes continued to run service 40 on Thursdays and summer Saturdays, the latter through to Minehead.

Another operator to appear in the area was Stenning from Merriott, who was awarded a contract in 1989 for an evening service from South Petherton to Yeovil via Martock and

Another Leyland Leopard/Plaxton Supreme Express, FDC 417V, came to Somerset from Cleveland Transit in the North East of England, already fitted with bus seats. (Author)

Montacute as well as a Tuesday and Friday shoppers' bus from South Petherton to Ilminster. These ran until 1992.

One of the less savoury aspects of bus deregulation manifested itself in the form of a severe competitive threat to Safeway, not as some might have expected from Southern National, but from Kingston Coaches of Yeovil. From 11 January 1988, trading as Yeovilian Bus Services, they started three routes. These were: 01 – Yeovil to South Petherton via West Coker, Crewkerne, Merriott and Hinton St George, 02 – Yeovil to South Petherton via Montacute and Stoke Sub Hamdon and 03 – Yeovil to South Petherton via Tintinhull, Martock and Bower Hinton. All running Mondays to Saturdays, the first two directly competed with the Safeway services while the third paralleled Southern National service 52. To run their new services, Kingston Coaches acquired four Leyland Nationals and a Bedford bus.

Safeway did not reduce their fares (which were already relatively low), but ran a few 'duplicates' on their services, and retained much of the customer loyalty. Yeovilian were charging about half of Safeway's and Southern National's fares and there were reports of buses racing each other to stops, just like the 1920s! Service 01 was withdrawn between Merriott and South Petherton and service 03 entirely in March 1988, but the remainder of 01 and 02 had to be suffered by Safeway until February 1990, with much worry over the company's future financial stability. It can probably be said that Miss Gunn emerged bruised but still in business, being well used to a fight!

On a brighter note, Safeway celebrated their sixtieth anniversary in March 1988 with the scaling down of Yeovilian operations, the issue of a model of Leyland Leopard PYC 746L for collectors, and with vehicles being adorned with lettering proudly proclaiming '1928-sixty years public service-1988'.

In 1993, Somerset County Council allocated numbers to the Safeway bus services. The Wednesday Taunton route was 603, the Friday bus to Ilminster and Yeovil was 680, the former H&C service from South Petherton/Crewkerne to Yeovil via Montacute the 681, and the original Safeway Yeovil via Crewkerne service the 682. Although the services were described thus in the Council's timetable booklets, it was mainly a paper exercise as the numbers rarely appeared on Safeway's own timetables or on the vehicles. The Friday shoppers' service from South Petherton to Ilminster and then on to Yeovil via Barrington and Kingsbury, was finally withdrawn after 1 July 1994, being uneconomic.

seventeen
A new era

Excavations by the water company resulted in the roadway being made too narrow at North Perrott for the usual vehicles to get by comfortably. There was a choice of a lengthy diversion, or the use of a smaller bus, so a twenty-three-seat Renault S56 with Northern Counties body was quickly purchased in April 1999 to alleviate the problem. Remaining in the white livery it arrived with, it had few supporters and was little used after the roadworks had finished.

For some years, Veronica Gunn's second cousin Vernon had been visiting South Petherton to carry out repairs and maintenance on the vehicles, as well as accompanying her on trips to dealers when she wished to inspect a bus or coach prior to purchase. He ran a car-dealing business at Pennymoor near Tiverton in Devon and would also go up to Somerset every alternate Sunday to take Miss Gunn out for a drive with lunch on the way.

The current proprietor of Safeway – Vernon Gunn, stands in front of Leyland Leopard NPA 228W. A mainstay of the bus services 1986-2003, this coach was originally part of the revitalised Green Line fleet introduced by London Country Bus Services. (Author)

After Vernon Gunn took over the business, his first purchase was another Leyland Leopard/Willowbrook Warrior, similar to GIB 5970. HIL 7772 was originally coach TPT 25V of 1980, re-bodied in 1991, and is picking up for Yeovil at Crewkerne. (Author)

Seventy years after there was a Dennis Dart in the Safeway fleet came another bus with that name, but looking somewhat different to the one in 1931! J601 KCU carries a Wright body and came from the Go Ahead North East group. The frontal signwriting is more appropriate for the supermarket chain rather than the South Petherton bus company, being incorrectly in the plural. It has since been rectified. (Author)

Safeway timetable display case in Crewkerne in 1999. (Author)

His knowledge and practical ability, together with the fact that he also was V. Gunn, possibly made Veronica decide that he should eventually be the proprietor of Safeway, and made plans accordingly.

In May 1999 Miss Gunn suffered a stroke and was taken to hospital in Yeovil. Her niece, Kay Jack (Herbert's daughter) then managed the business in her absence. However, Veronica died in the local South Petherton hospital on 18 August, at the age of 91 and Vernon Gunn was confirmed as the new owner of Safeway Services. South Petherton had lost what could well have been its oldest member of the business community, but also somebody well known for supporting charities and the Church. Local organisations had benefited from her extremely benevolent coach-hire rates for their outings. She once said 'I've never wanted a lot of money – that you have to leave behind.'

Vernon Gunn now devotes most of his working time to Safeway, commuting from his home near Cullompton in east Devon. Although his first vehicle acquisition as new owner was another Leyland Leopard with a Willowbrook Warrior bus body, purchased in February 2000, some Volvo B10M vehicles and a Dennis Dart bus with Wright bodywork have entered the fleet over the last three years, replacing some of the Leylands. One of the Volvos (G997 OKK) was painted in an eye-catching orange and yellow coach livery which Vernon Gunn has introduced, but the Dart is reassuringly in traditional red, cream and maroon. The fleet currently stands at thirteen – three Leopards, three Tigers, four Volvos, two DAFs and the Dart, in addition to the old Dennis Lancet which is presently in store in the garage.

On taking over, Vernon Gunn was obliged to raise the bus fares – the first increase for five years, as well as seeking realistic rates for school contract services, to ensure Safeway's survival. Revised timetables were introduced on the Yeovil services from 30 October 2000,

The last four years has seen a partial modernisation of the coach fleet, with four Volvo B10Ms. K835 HUM, with Jonckheere body, was the first and has been operated in an all-white livery. (Author)

This Volvo with Caetano body, purchased in 2000, was painted in an experimental new coach livery of yellow and orange. (Author)

When seen reversing at North Street corner, South Petherton, *en route* from Crewkerne to Yeovil in July 2003, Safeway's Volvo/East Lancs bus NIB 8459 was still in the grey and blue livery of its previous operator – Buffalo of Flitwick, Beds. (Author)

requiring one less vehicle, and the routes are now covered by three 'all day' buses with a fourth in use for short periods. Odcombe is now served only by a morning peak-hour journey to Yeovil while a reduced Saturday service is run on the original Gunn route to Crewkerne and Yeovil. As mentioned earlier, extremely low patronage on the Wednesday Taunton service brought about its withdrawal in March 2001, despite the recent receipt of some funding from the County Council. However, at the time of going to press, the Yeovil routes are still mainly run commercially. While Vernon Gunn has not ruled out future bidding for Somerset County Council bus service contracts, if the price is right, nothing he has seen so far for local routes has tempted him.

So, as a new century begins, it is business as usual at North Street garage. Inevitably, things will change and new vehicle types will appear in time, as the Leylands become more expensive to maintain and operate. Yet for now, the roar of the Leopard or Tiger can still be heard reverberating off the walls of the hamstone buildings which hug the streets in the villages served by Safeway. It is no doubt comforting to the bus users and the private hire and excursion customers that the business is still upholding its traditions and values of reliable, personal service, to the same dictums practised by Bert and Vera Gunn. It would not be advisable to speculate on the future as so much can happen in the bus and coach industry in a quite short period of time, but one must hope that Safeway services remain a familiar sight on the roads of south Somerset and elsewhere for a long time to come.

Appendix 1
Lists of staff members
(as can be recalled)

Hutchings & Cornelius

Drivers
Gordon Baker
Reg Beale
Jack Bindon
Sam Blackwell
Fred Bridge
Charlie Brown
Les Burfield
Reg Burrows
Harry Coles
Rex Corbet
Charlie Cornelius
Len Cornelius
Charlie Dare
Bert Down
Howard Drayton
Arthur Edmonds
Pete Elswood
Ron Fuller
George Gamble
George Gentle
Bert Gass
Harold Guard
Arthur Harris
Ken Harvey
Stan Harwood
Vic Higgins
Ian Holmes
Len Hooper
Stewart Jacobs
Stuart Jackson
Ken Jones
Marlowe Male

Arthur Martin
Phil Masters
Herbie Meade
Fred Morris
Andy Naismith
Malcolm Neville
Dick Osborne
George Rowley
Ken Sole
Cyril Thorne
Fred Virgin
Mickey Walker
Bill Warren
Cyril Welch
Fred Welch
Mike Welfare
John Willey
Dennis Winter
Joe Wrenn

Conductors/Conductresses
Bertie Attwell
Frank Bell
Ned Best (became driver)
Harold Brister
Jim Brooks
Jim Callow
Harold Dabinett
Edna Dinham
Sid England
Brenda England
Eddie Farrell
Ena Foot

Ruby Foot
Maisie Goodall
John Gundry (became driver)
Bill Harwood
Ken Heathman
Daisy Keetch
Phyllis Langford
Peggy Langford
Olga Lee
Ella Lock
Betty Louch
Iris Male
George Marsh
Yvonne Pond
Harry Quantock (became driver)
Dick Ryder
Joan Smith
Phillip Stenner
Bill Taylor
Ernie Welch

Mechanics/Drivers
John Brake
Len Legg
Dennis Single
Bernard Welch

Office
Fred Alford
Stanley Baker
David Grimmett
Christine Hodgkinson

Safeway Services

*Drivers_*
Jack Apers
Eddie Beer
Jack Bindon (fr om H&C)
Les Brown
Jack Bryce (also mechanic)
Graham Butler
Ted Callow
Charlie Cornelius (from H&C)
Howard Drayton (from H&C)
David Dodge
Ian Foulds
Joe Frost (also mechanic)
Bert Goss
John Gundry (from H&C)

Merv Hallett
John Hillier (also mechanic)
Colin Irish
Ivor Kay
Leon Keetch
Bill Leverick
Paul March
Roy Markham
Richard Matravers
Rob McGill
Rex Meare (also mechanic)
John Osborne
Brian Pettifor
Eddie Reave
Eric Rice
Gary Rodgers
Jeff Rogers

Rodney Shepherd
Shaun Tett
Bob Tomlin
Nigel Tucker
Alf White
John White
Stan Williams
Dennis Winter (from H&C)

Conductresses
Cissie Gayleard
Gladys Gunn
Ivy Williams

Office
Christine Hodgkinson (from H&C)

Appendix 2
Fleet Lists

Notes on codes used to describe vehicle bodies

The standard codes as recognised in most enthusiasts publications have been used to describe body types and seating capacities.

Prefix

B	Single Deck bus
C	Single Deck coach
DP	Single Deck Dual Purpose vehicle
FB	Single Deck Forward Control or half-cab bus with flat fronted body
FC	Single Deck Forward Control or half-cab coach with flat fronted body
L	Lowbridge Double Deck (with sunken side gangway upstairs)
H	Highbridge (or normal height for that type) Double Deck

Figures
Seating capacities as stated

Suffix

C	Centre entrance
F	Front or Forward entrance
R	Rear entrance (with open platform on double-deckers)
RD	Rear entrance with platform doors (on double-deckers)

Safeway Services

Regn No.	Chassis	Body	Date in	Former Owner	Date out	Disposal	Note
YC 2376	Dennis G	Waveney	B20F	03/28	New	05/35	Pearman, London SE5 (Lorry)	
XV 5430	Dennis G	Waveney	B18F	?/28	New		Untraced	
YD 1728	Dennis Dart	Strachan	B20F	03/31	New	06/37	Alexander, Horsham	
YD 45	Dennis Lancet 1	Dennis	B32R	05/34	New	06/50	Scrapped	
PL 3022	Dennis GL	Strachan	B20F	by 04/36	Locke, Guildford		Untraced	
CYA 105	Dennis Lancet 1	Dennis	DP32R	10/36	New	05/53	Untraced	
EYB 711	Dennis Pike	Dennis	C20F	06/39	New	08/57	Mobile Shop	
RV 1494	TSM C60A7	Harrington	C32R	01/42	Sprackling, Blandford	06/50	Scrapped	
FYD 132	Bedford OWB	Duple	B32F	01/43	New	08/58	Scrapped	1
FYD 983	Bedford OWB	Duple	B32F	11/43	New	08/58	Scrapped	
GYC 330	Bedford OB	Duple	B32F	03/46	New	12/62	Racing Car Transporter, Brighton	
FOT 432	Bedford OB	Wadham	C27F	08/48	Creamline, Bordon	07/64	Talbot, Moreton in Marsh	
ETP 184	Dennis Lancet J3	Reading	C33F	06/49	New			2
FYD 922	Bedford OWB	Duple	B30F	11/49	Fursland, Bridgwater	07/59	Mobile Shop	
MYB 33	Bedford OB	Duple	C29F	10/50	New	11/74	Piggott, Weymouth (Preserved)	
TYD 755	AEC Reliance MU3RV	Duple	C43F	06/55	New	09/78	Scrapped	

Regn No.	Chassis	Body		Date in	Former Owner	Date out	Disposal	Note
MVA 832	Bedford SBO	Duple Midland	B40F	01/59	Heybrook Bay M.S., Downthomas	05/73	Mears, Wells (Preserved)	3
PXC 539	Bedford SBG	Owen	B36R	07/59	Super, Upminster	01/61	Smith, Rickmansworth	
600 GYC	Karrier BF3023	Reading	C14F	05/60	New	05/74	Benson & Ewelme British Legion, via ?	
UPK 615	Bedford SBO	Duple Midland	B38F	01/61	Safeguard, Guildford	08/75	Untraced	4
200 APB	AEC Reliance MU3RV	Burlingham	B44F	11/62	Safeguard, Guildford	04/82	Jones, Swansea (Preserved)	
LBK 766	Bedford SBG	Duple	C36F	01/64	Giles, South Petherton	06/69	Edwards, Beddau	
SOR 117	Bedford SB3	Duple	C37F	01/64	Giles, South Petherton	02/80	Millman, Buckfastleigh	
7718 HK	Bedford SB3	Duple	C41F	07/64	Welling, Burton	03/75	Scrapped	
399 DLD	Bedford SB8	Harrington	C41F	06/69	Seward, Dalwood	08/81	Pearce, Darch & Willcox, Cattistock	
PYC 746L	Leyland Leopard PSU3B/4R	Willowbrook	DP51F	04/73	New	by 10/97	Untraced	5
RYA 676L	Leyland Leopard PSU3B/4R	Willowbrook	B51F	05/73	New	09/93	Scrapped	
WYD 397M	Volvo B58	Plaxton	C51F	05/74	New	by 02/85	Dartington & Totnes O.C.,Totnes	
TYD 888	AEC Reliance MU3RV	Duple	C43F	05/74	Wake, Sparkford	12/79	W of Eng Transport Collection, Winkleigh (Preserved)	
UAR 940M	Leyland Leopard PSU3B/4R	Plaxton	C53F	02/78	Grant, Fareham	12/99	Stock Car Transporter	6
HPG 30N	Leyland Leopard PSU3B/4R	Duple	C49F	10/78	Safeguard, Guildford	by 10/92	Untraced	

Regn No.	Chassis	Body		Date in	Former Owner	Date out	Disposal	Note
FPC 15J	AEC Reliance 6MU4R	Willowbrook	B51F	04/79	H&C, South Petherton	by 06/87	Nightingale, Exmouth	
TYC 250G	AEC Reliance 6MU3R	Willowbrook	B45F	06/79	H&C, South Petherton	03/86	Phillips, Port Talbot (Preserved)	
WYD 306H	AEC Reliance 6MU3R	Willowbrook	B45F	06/79	H&C, South Petherton	12/81	Clifton College, Bristol	
NYD 440L	Bristol LH6L	ECW	B43F	06/79	H&C, South Petherton	by 05/84	Hillier, Foxham	
AUA 436J	AEC Reliance 6U3ZR	Plaxton	C53F	06/79	Eagle, Bristol	08/79	Maisey, Church Village	
LNY 765L	Leyland Leopard PSU3B/4R	Plaxton	C53F	08/79	Morris, Pencoed	04/83	Walters, Crumlin	
PXS 820N	Ford R1114	Willowbrook	B53F	04/80	Graham, Paisley	08/86	Coachcraft, Armthorpe	
TYD 911W	Leyland Leopard PSU3F/5R	Duple	B61F	11/80	New	05/01	Specialised Transport Training, Liverpool	7
VYC 852W	Leyland Leopard PSU3F/5R	Duple	C53F	04/81	New	by 03/03	Beadles, Newtown	
AML 614H	AEC Merlin 4P2R	Metro Cammell	B50F	12/81	London Transport	06/89	Allmey, Eastcote	
YYA 122X	Leyland Leopard PSU3F/5R	Plaxton	C53F	07/82	New			
VPF 42M	Leyland Leopard PSU3B/4R	Willowbrook	B53F	by 12/82	Safeguard, Guildford	by 03/95	Untraced	
A983 NYC	Leyland Tiger TRCTL11/2R	Plaxton	C53F	08/83	New			
OGR 654P	Leyland Leopard PSU3C/4R	Willowbrook	B55F	07/84	Ford, Ackworth	08/92	Plaxton, Stanton Wick (Dealer)	
C744 JYA	Leyland Tiger TRCTL11/3RZ	Willowbrook	C55F	07/86	New	03/02	Donald, Henstridge	

Regn No.	Chassis	Body	Date in	Former Owner	Date out	Disposal	Note
NPA 228W	Leyland Leopard PSU3F/4R	Plaxton	C49F	by 09/86	London Country	05/03	Scrapped	
E565 YYA	Leyland Tiger TRCT11L/3RZ	Duple	C55F	04/88	New			
FHA 609Y	Leyland Tiger TRCTL11/2R	Duple	C49F	12/91	Ludlow, Halesowen	08/93	Felix, Stanley	8
GIB 5970	Leyland Leopard PSU3E/4R	Willowbrook	B48F	04/92	Kellett, Barnoldswick			9
F202 HSO	Leyland Tiger TRCTL11/3ARZM	Plaxton	C53F	05/93	Park, Hamilton			
HHU 42V	Leyland Leopard PSU3E/4R	Plaxton	C49F	09/93	Evans, Bedminster	08/01	Wacton, Bromyard (Scrapped)	10
FDC 417V	Leyland Leopard PSU3E/4R	Plaxton	B53F	09/94	Cleveland Transit	03/02	Rexquote, Norton Fitzwarren	11
HFG 207T	Leyland Leopard PSU3E/4R	Plaxton	C53F	08/96	Cross Country, Castle Eaton	08/00	Wacton, Bromyard (Scrapped)	12
F340 VEF	Renault S56	Northern Counties	B23F	04/99	Holt, Thornton-Le-Dale	09/99	Untraced Non-PSV	
HIL 7772	Leyland Leopard PSU3E/4R	Willowbrook	B48F	02/00	Alexcars, Cirencester	11/03	Scrapped	13
K835 HUM	Volvo B10M-60	Jonckheere	C50F	03/00	Burton, Haverhill			
G997 OKK	Volvo B10M-60	Caetano	C53F	09/00	Wilson, Strathaven	12/02	Baker, Duloe	
J601 KCU	Dennis Dart 9.8SDL	Wright	B40F	04/01	Go Coastline			
RJI 3046	Volvo B10M-61	Duple	C51F	08/01	Kingdom, Tiverton			14
YXI 9258	Volvo B10M-61	Van Hool	C53F	03/02	Skill, Nottingham			15
NIB 8459	Volvo B10M-61	East Lancs	B55F	05/02	Buffalo, Flitwick			16

Regn No.	Chassis	Body		Date in	Former Owner	Date out	Disposal	Note
ELZ 2062	DAF SB2305	Jonckheere	C51Ft	12/02	Hemmings, Torrington			17
OWO 235Y	Leyland Leopard PSU3G/2R	Duple	DP53F	08/03	Smith, Pylle			
A710 SDV	DAF SB2300	Plaxton	C53F	11/03	Redwood, Hemyock			18

Notes:

1   reseated to B30F

2   withdrawn 07/69 and retained for preservation. Re-registered ASV 900

3   converted to SB8 and reseated to B39F

4   converted to SB8

5   reseated to B53F

6   reseated to B53F

7   reseated to B59F

8   originally registered YPD 137Y then GJI 2223

9   originally registered XCW 153R. Original Willowbrook coach body removed in 1992 prior to acquisition

10   originally registered KUB 555V then HHF 15. Reseated to B53F

11   fitted with bus seats in coach body when acquired

12   originally registered BYJ 919T then 423 DCD

13   originally registered TPT 25V.   Original Willowbrook coach body removed 11/91

14   originally registered RMU 967Y

15   originally registered F751 ENE

16   originally registered E637 NEL. Original fire-damaged coach body removed 1991

17   originally registered G975LRP

18   originally registered A546 RVH then PIL 6501 then USV 630

T. Hutchings and A. Cornelius - Lists of Vehicles Owned

T. Hutchings

Regn No.	Chassis	Body	Date in	Former Owner	Date out	Disposal	Note
YA 4505	Chevrolet 21hp	8	12/22	New		Untraced	
YB 895	Chevrolet 22hp	14	02/25	New	01/28	Cornelius, Barrington	
YC 1389	Thornycroft A2L	B20F	11/27	New	05/34	Hutchings& Cornelius, South Petherton	
YB 895	Chevrolet 22hp	14	05/28	Cornelius, Barrington	11/28	Untraced	
YC 4558	Thornycroft A1	Hall Lewis B14F	11/28	New	05/34	Hutchings & Cornelius, South Petherton	
YC 6604	Thornycroft A6	26	06/29	New	05/34	Hutchings & Cornelius, South Petherton	
YC 7987	Thornycroft BC	Ransomes C32F	12/29	New	05/34	Hutchings & Cornelius, South Petherton	

A. Cornelius

Regn No.	Chassis	Body	Date in	Former Owner	Date out	Disposal	Note
YB 895	Chevrolet 22hp	14	01/28	Hutching, South Petherton	05/28	Hutchings, South Petherton	
YC 3058	Thornycroft A2	Vincent B20F	05/28	New		Glanville, Taunton	
YC 7167	Chevrolet LQ	Marks B14F	08/29	New	05/34	Watts, Isle Brewers	
YD 374	TRhornycroft A2	Vincent B20F	07/30	New	05/34	Hutchings & Cornelius, South Petherton	
YD 2764	Thornycroft A2	Vincent B20F	07/31	New	05/34	Hutchings & Cornelius, South Petherton	
YD 4044	Thornycroft Cygnet	Beadle B30R	02/32	New	05/34	Hutchings & Cornelius, South Petherton	
YD 7317	Dennis Lancet 1	Dennis C32R	06/33	New	05/34	Hutchings & Cornelius, South Petherton	

Hutchings & Cornelius Services Ltd

Petherton

Regn No.	Chassis	Body	Date in	Former Owner	Date out	Disposal	Note
YC 1389	Thornycroft A2L	B20F	05/34	Hutchings, South Petherton	?/38	Untraced	
YC 4558	Thornycroft A1	Hall Lewis B14F	05/34	Hutchings, South Petherton	09/39	Converted to lorry	
YC 6604	Thornycroft A6	B26F	05/34	Hutchings, South Petherton	?/38	Untraced	
YC 7987	Thornycroft BC	Ransomes C32F	05/34	Hutchings, South Petherton	06/48	Converted to lorry	
YD 374	Thornycroft A2	Vincent B20F	05/34	Cornelius, Barrington	12/43	Untraced	
YD 2764	Thornycroft A2	Vincent B20F	05/34	Cornelius, Barrington	05/43	Untraced	
YD 4044	Thornycroft Cygnet	Beadle B32R	05/34	Cornelius, Barrington	?/46	Untraced	
YD 7317	Dennis Lancet 1	Dennis C32R	05/34	Cornelius, Barrington	07/49	Untraced	
YD 9639	Thornycroft Cygnet	Beadle B32R	05/34	Thornycroft demonstrator	10/50	Untraced	
AYA 170	Dennis Ace	Dennis B20F	07/34	New	07/42	Kemp, Woodcote	
AYC 385	Dennis Mace	Dennis B26C	03/35	New	by 02/52	National Coal Board	
AOR 147	Thornycroft Dainty	Wadham B20F	06/35	New	10/50	Sparshatt, Southampton (Dealer)	
BYD 182	Thornycroft Dainty	Grose FC25F	07/36	New	07/49	Untraced	
CYC 422	Dennis Arrow Minor	Dennis C25F	06/37	New	04/55	Untraced	1

Regn No.	Chassis	Body	B...	Date in	Former Owner	Date out	Disposal	Note
CYC 657	Dennis Arrow Minor	Dennis	B26F	06/37	New	06/53	Untraced	
KX 6535	Dennis GL	Dennis	B20F	?/37	Osborne, Aylesbury	?/38	Unknown Dealer (Scrap)	
EYD 220	Dennis Lancet 2	Duple	C33F	11/39	New	05/58	Untraced	
KX 9458	Bedford WLB	Duple	B20F	06/40	Red Rose, Aylesbury	06/49	Untraced	
EBB 349	Bedford WTB	Northern C/Builders	C26F	07/40	Summerson, West Auckland	01/52	Untraced	
CUP 282	Dennis Lancet 2	Duple	B32F	05/41		01/62	Isaac, Lufton (Scrap)	2
FN 9948	Tilling Stevens B10C2	Short	B29R	?/42	Wake, Sparkford	by 06/48	Showman	
FYD 137	Bedford OWB	Duple	B32F	01/43	New	11/67	Coles, Barwick (Scrap)	3
FYD 138	Bedford OWB	Mulliner	B32F	01/43	New	06/55	Hatton, Culmstock	
BTE 861	Dennis Lancet 2	Duple	C32F	02/43		by 08/58	Untraced	4
JJ 1836	Dennis Lancet 1	Duple	C32R	03/43	War Department	08/48	Untraced	
AHU 450	Thornycroft Cygnet	Beadle	C32R	05/43	War Department	08/48	Pearce, Hanham	
AMR 733	Dennis Lancet 2	Ashby	B33F	08/43	Cully, Salisbury	04/56	Jeffs, Bridport	5
CHU 966	Thornycroft Lightning	Bence	FC26R	02/46	War Department	11/47	Untraced	
ANY 500	Dennis Lancet 1	D.J. Davies	C32C	06/46	RAF	06/50	Sparshatt, Southampton (Dealer)	
JPK 803	Bedford OWB	Mulliner	B30F	06/47	Hayter, Guildford	04/57	Untraced	
BRP 835	Bedford OWB	Roe	B32F	12/47	York Bros., Northampton	05/52	Untraced	
JYD 426	Bedford OB	Mulliner	B31F	03/48	New	04/61	Unknown Dealer (Scrap)	6
KYA 238	Dennis Lancet J3	Lee	C33F	07/48	New	12/65	Coles, Barwick (Scrap)	7

123

Regn No.	Chassis	Body		Date in	Former Owner	Date out	Disposal	Note
KYD 379	Seddon Mk IV	Associated C/Builders	C29F	04/49	New	08/62	Coles, Barwick (Scrap)	
LYC 10	Bedford OB	Mulliner	B31F	11/49	New	01/63	Untraced	8
LYC 129	Austin CXB	Reading	C31F	01/50	New	12/65	Vincent Finance, Yeovil	9
MYA 391	Jensen	Sparshatts	B40F	07/50	New	02/64	Coles, Barwick (Scrap)	10
MYA 816	Jensen	Sparshatts	B40F	08/50	New	12/64	Coles, Barwick (Scrap)	
CCX 660	Daimler CWA6	Brush	L55R	07/53	Huddersfield	09/57	Scrapped by H&C	
RYD 143	Austin CXD	Strachan	FC32C	06/54	New	01/64	Coles, Barwick (Scrap)	
RYD 144	Dennis Lancet LU2	Strachan	B44F	06/54	New	03/67	Coles, Barwick (Scrap)	
TYC 319	Dennis Lancet LU2	Strachan	DP41F	04/55	New	11/69	Coles, Stalbridge (Scrap)	
TYC 320	Dennis Lancet LU2	Strachan	DP41F	04/55	New	12/68	Coles, Stalbridge (Scrap)	
RC 8482	Daimler CWA6	Duple	L55R	04/57	Trent	10/58	Unknown Dealer (Scrap)	
YYB 117	Dennis Lancet LU2	Harrington	DP40F	07/57	New	12/71	Smith Vehicle Recovery	
YYB 118	Dennis Lancet LU2	Harrington	B42F	08/57	New	09/74	Tor Coaches, Street	
YYB 119	Dennis Lancet LU2	Harrington	B42F	09/57	New	09/73	Preservation Group, Guildford	
623 BYA	Dennis Loline 1	East Lancs	H68RD	06/58	New	07/73	Sykes, Barnsley (Dealer)	11
708 BYB	Austin J2/VA	Kenex	11	06/58	New	02/65	Untraced	
122 BYD	Austin J2/VA	Kenex	11	11/58	New	04/65	Untraced	
632 CYB	Dennis Lancet LU5	Harrington	DP40F	12/58	New	01/73	Untraced	
823 KYD	AEC Reliance 2MU3RV	Harrington	C37F	06/61	New	05/69	Blackford, Isleworth	
933 NYB	Albion Nimbus NS3AN	Harrington	B31F	04/62	New	10/70	Foster, Ellesmere Port	
934 NYB	Albion Nimbus NS3AN	Harrington	B31F	04/62	New	10/70	Westmoreland Hire, Kendal	

Regn No.	Chassis	Body		Date in	Former Owner	Date out	Disposal	Note
432 RYD	Albion Nimbus NS3AN	Harrington	B31F	01/63	New	08/70	Miller, Lanark	
217 UYC	AEC Reliance 2MU3RA	Harrington	B45F	12/63	New	10/72	Knubley, Bruton	
216 UYC	AEC Reliance 2MU3RA	Harrington	C41F	03/64	New	06/70	Wake, Sparkford	
BYD 730C	Austin J2/M16	BMC	11	02/65	New	08/68	Untraced	
BYD 735C	AEC Reliance 4MU4RA	Harrington	C51F	04/65	New	10/74	Temple, Up Hatherley	
CYD 724C	AEC Reliance 2MU4RA	Harrington	C41F	07/65	New	04/79	Taylor, Tintinhull	
YMP 551	Bedford SB	Duple	C37F	06/67	Hill, Stibb Cross	09/69	Coles, Stalbridge (Scrap)	
KHU 629E	Bedford CALZ	Martin Walter	11	08/68	Cattermole, Bristol	02/70	Sidford Car Sales, Southampton	
TYC 250G	AEC Reliance 6MU3R	Willowbrook	B45F	12/68	New	05/79	Gunn, South Petherton	
TYD 122G	AEC Reliance 6MU3R	Willowbrook	B45F	03/69	New	05/79	Tillingbourne, Gomshall	
VYA 834G	AEC Reliance 6MU4R	Plaxton	C41F	05/69	New	03/74	Ladvale, Cheltenham	
WYD 306H	AEC Reliance 6MU3R	Willowbrook	B45F	11/69	New	05/79	Gunn, South Petherton	
WYD 928H	AEC Reliance 6MU3R	Willowbrook	B45F	11/69	New	05/79	Knubley, Bruton	
CYA 181J	AEC Reliance 6MU3R	Plaxton	B47F	12/70	New	05/79	Knubley, Bruton	
GYC 160K	Bristol LH6L	ECW	B45F	01/72	New	10/77	Pirt, Dorking	

Regn No.	Chassis	Body		Date in	Former Owner	Date out	Disposal	Note
KYA 905K	AEC Reliance 6MU4R	Willowbrook	C51F	08/72	New	12/77	Garelochhead Coach Service	
NYD 440L	Bristol LH6L	ECW	B43F	01/73	New	05/79	Gunn, South Petherton	
RYA 700L	Bristol VRTSL6LX	ECW	H70F	06/73	New	05/79	West Wales, Tycroes	
GWY 970J	Ford R226	Plaxton	C53F	10/73	Finsbury, London EC1	07/75	Elcock & Prince, Ironbridge	
UYD 920M	Ford R1014	Plaxton	C45F	03/74	New	05/79	Seaview, Parkstone	
EMB 167K	Ford R226	Plaxton	C53F	09/74	Shearing, Altrincham	05/76	Foster, Glastonbury	
JYB 538N	Ford R1014	Plaxton	B46F	04/75	New	05/79	Wimpey (Contractor)	
KYA 386N	Ford R1114	Duple	C53F	06/75	New	05/79	Wyness, Poole	
OYC 241P	Ford R1114	Plaxton	C53F	04/76	New	04/79	Barry, Weymouth	
XTM 875L	Ford R192	Duple	C45F	05/76	Edwards, Markham	01/79	Hehir, Kilkenny, Eire	
995 OHW	Bedford SB5	Duple	C41F	06/76	Wessex, Bristol	01/77	Ball, Plymouth	
SGD 654	Leyland Atlantean	Alexander	H78F	10/76	Greater Glasgow PTE	01/79	Unknown Dealer (Scrap)	
FPC 15J	AEC Reliance 6MU4R	Willowbrook	B51F	09/77	Safeguard, Guildford	04/79	Gunn, South Petherton	
GST 423N	Ford R1014	Duple	B53F	11/77	Newton, Dingwall	05/79	Wimpey (Contractor)	
JUN 199P	Ford R1014	Duple	C45F	12/78	Lovering, Combe Martin	05/79	Pearson, Bournemouth	
DAU 427C	Leyland Atlantean	Metro Cammell	H77F	01/79	Nottingham	05/79	Tor Coaches, Street	

Notes

1   possibly used by War Department 1939-1945

2   rebodied by Vincent as FB37F

3   reseated to B30F, then rebodied by Vincent as B28F

4   reseated to C33F

5   possibly acquired via War Department

6   rebuilt by Vincent as B29F

7   rebodied by Vincent as FB33F

8   rebuilt by Vincent as B29F

9   reseated to C27F

10   reseated to B39F

11   subsequently exported to Italy

Other local titles published by Tempus

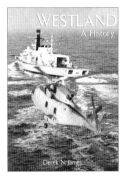

Westland: A History
DEREK N. JAMES

In 1915, the owner of the Petter oil engin company built an aircraft factory in Yeovil. Taking advantage of the hundreds of sub-contracts being handed out, the company he founded, known simply as Westland, began the manufacture of aircraft under licence from Sopwith. From these beginnings grew Europe's largest manufacturer of helicopters. Westland is still with us, albeit combined with Agusta of Italy, and the pioneering spirit of the founders is still with the company to this day.
0 7524 2772 5

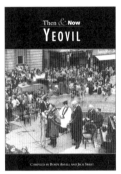

Yeovil: Then & Now
ROBIN ANSELL & JACK SWEET

Yeovil's changing face is expertly documented in this fascinating collection of over seventy-five paired photographs. The images range in date from one of the earliest surviving street scenes, taken in the 1860s, to the ubiquitous postcard views of the early twentieth-century townscape. If the Yeovil of today and yesterday interests you, then this new book deserves a place on your bookshelf!
0 7524 2646 X

British Built Aircraft South-west and Central Southern England
RON SMITH

The second volume in Ron Smith's encyclopedia of British-built aircraft, covering every manufacturer of aircraft in southern England from Hampshire to Cornwall, Gloucester and Somerset. The definitive reference work for those interested in aircraft construction in Britain, British Built Aircraft covers the manufacturers at Southampton, Farnborough, the Isle of Wight, Yeovil, Bristol and Gloucester as well as a myriad of sub-contractors and one-off designs.
0 7524 2785 7

Somerset County Cricket Club Classics
EDDIE LAWRENCE

Somerset's CCC have played over 2,400 matches since their admittance into the County Championship in 1891. This book covers fifty of the most memorable first-ckass matches over the 110 years of their history. Some of the greatest cricketers who have played for the club are recalled, including the three legends Viv Richards, Ian Botham and Joel Garner. This book is essential reading for all fans of Somerset CCC - it is bound to stir up memories of those unforgettable matches.
0 7524 2409 2

To discover more Tempus titles please visit us at:
www.tempus-publishing.com